Performance Auditing of Public Sector Property Contracts

Performance Auditing of Public Sector Property Contracts

LORI KEATING
PFI Compliance, UK

Routledge
Taylor & Francis Group

LONDON AND NEW YORK

First published in paperback 2024

First published 2011 by Gower Publishing

Published 2016 by Routledge
4 Park Square, Milton Park, Abingdon, Oxon OX14 4RN

and by Routledge
605 Third Avenue, New York, NY 10158

Routledge is an imprint of the Taylor & Francis Group, an informa business

© 2011, 2016, 2024 Lori Keating

The right of Lori Keating to be identified as author of this work has been asserted in accordance with sections 77 and 78 of the Copyright, Designs and Patents Act 1988.

Publisher's Note
The publisher has gone to great lengths to ensure the quality of this reprint but points out that some imperfections in the original copies may be apparent.

British Library Cataloguing in Publication Data
Keating, Lori.
  Performance auditing of public sector property contracts.
  1. Public contracts--Auditing. 2. Contracting out--
  Auditing. 3. Construction contracts--Auditing. 4. Public
  administration--Evaluation.
  I. Title
  657.8'335045-dc22

Library of Congress Cataloging-in-Publication Data
Keating, Lori.
  Performance auditing of public sector property contracts / by Lori Keating.
    p. cm.
  Includes bibliographical references and index.
  ISBN 978-0-566-08999-2 (hardback)
  1. Public contracts--Accounting. I. Title   .
  HF5686.P923K43 2010
  352.5'32439--dc22

                                                                    2010040072

ISBN: 978-0-566-08999-2 (hbk)
ISBN: 978-1-03-283830-4 (pbk)
ISBN: 978-1-315-59992-2 (ebk)

DOI: 10.4324/9781315599922

Contents

List of Figures

Acknowledgements

This book owes much to two important people: Barrie Ellis-Jones, who is central and fundamental to the entirety of my life; and Gerald Francis Keating, who has provided a fine model of how to work and live.

Profound thanks to John Tresham, John Hinchliffe, Ian Catlow, David Goldstone and Stephen Horne.

This book draws heavily from my experiences, and those of my colleagues, of performance auditing for the public sector over 15 years. While its backbone is a strong foundation in public sector policy, the lessons I might have to give are based on a large number of audits undertaken over a long period of time. The book is partially experiential, and based on good government policy.

All examples and hypotheses contained throughout this book are simply that, and non-specific to any particular contract. Any anecdotes are generic and are a blend from a variety of incidents experienced over time by a variety of people. All public sector policy requirements have influenced this book, and any mistake in their interpretation is strictly mine, and not of the foundation sources themselves. Any other mistakes are not due to the quality of my advisers and colleagues, but entirely attributable to my own negligence in taking their advice fully on board.

Introduction

'Auditors aren't boring people, we just get excited about stupid things.'
American joke

Webster's English Dictionary describes an audit as' ... any thorough examination and evaluation of a problem'. Audits can also discover a problem before it arises and be a proactive management device. Audits can look at performance, contractual compliance, legislative/statutory compliance, and can look at any micro or macro area of any contract to discover and evaluate any of these aspects overall, or in any kind of minute detail. Audits need not be 100 per cent thorough, in terms of understanding every aspect of every problem every time, but will always be concerned with independent and accurate problem assessment and evaluation.

Auditors wear the white hats in the cowboy movies of yore, and this book is meant to be a practical guide to performance auditing for public sector property managers and a series of guidelines for auditors of public sector property contracts. The book almost entirely concentrates on FM (Facilities Management) Contracts, rather than construction, though techniques outlined within the book can be used in construction contracts as well. FM Contracts, with lifespans of 5–25 years, and that cover a widely diverse series of deliverables, demand particular skill-sets to understand if the contract is performing as expected, and as contractually required.

To stress, this book talks about performance auditing, as distinct from financial auditing. While performance auditing can also naturally look at the financial aspects of any property contract, the majority of this type of audit work is concerned with how functions are being carried out according to contractual requirements. Encarta defines 'performance' as 'the manner in which something or somebody functions, operates or behaves', and the broad definition works for this book. The subject of performance auditing is no less complicated than for financial audits and examinations. Performance auditing aims to look at the degree to which a series of complex discrete subjects operates within the parameters required of it – be they contractual, legislative, good practice, or common sense. Performance auditing of public sector contracts is meant to see if a building or an estate is functioning as it should and if not, why not.

The book makes no particular distinction between FM Contracts and operational-phase PFI Contracts. The differences between the two – the increased longevity and the complexity of monitoring/financial arrangements in PFI contracts – has no fundamental impact on carrying out any kind of performance audit.

PFI Contracts are vastly more complex than those FM Contracts which are simply let to deliver a number of services, and where the ownership and direct line management is meant to remain firmly in the public sector's hands. The only difference to an auditor between looking at a traditional FM contract and a PFI Contract is the amount of time needed to understand the contract, its expectations and deliverables, and the reality of service delivery 'on the ground'. All building/FM Contracts of whatever type are let to the private sector so that they can relieve a detailed management burden from the public sector, and which are expected to deliver a quality service at a price that demonstrably represents Value For Money. Given these overarching similarities, then, throughout the book we simply talk about FM on the whole, which includes PFI.

This book discusses all aspects of performance auditing of public sector property contracts. Auditing is a specialist skill, and auditors bring different techniques and mindsets and specialist knowledge to any audit assignment. The book does not give away all auditor 'tricks' or techniques, but aims to show how different strategies can assist the evaluation of different aspects of any one problem at any one time. This book does show how auditors do work in a broad sense, and so provides a guide for any professional looking for guidance, or for the public sector looking to understand further what is possible in an audit situation.

Audits are a public sector right, and a matter of good management sense. Audits are often used to assure contract managers that their perceptions are demonstrably true. Audits present unambiguous non-debateable facts so that management decisions can be taken pragmatically and clearly. Audits can be a positive tool, embraced by both the public and private sectors, as a way of clearly informing ongoing management decisions as to progress, resources required, and all other minutiae of effective contract management.

A good audit will tell a complete factual story of the subject under consideration and place any problem discovered squarely in the matrix of contractual compliance. Any good audit will look for successes in the subject, as well as areas that might be doing less well. A good audit instruction will take care that the appointed auditor remains independent, and free to come to his own conclusions. The independence of the audit process should always be sacrosanct, and this independence as a base concept informs all subjects throughout this book.

A one-off audit, or an audit regime, is a basic business tool that can help drive good management by all parties to any property contract. The thorough examination of any problem can be of fundamental use in saving money, maintaining Health and Safety compliance, improving service delivery and, in the case of the public sector, an audit regime does help in discharging public sector accountability requirements.

The book will follow an audit process from commencement to conclusion, and contains discussion of factors that contribute to the success of any audit.

Key Concepts and Definitions

Introduction

This chapter provides an introduction to the cornerstones of public sector audit. For those new to Facilities Management/building contracts, this section will define some of the technical terms used throughout the book. For those who are expert in the field, this brief section can be used as an aide-mémoire.

Brief Definitions and List of Abbreviations

Facilities Management or FM: The management of a building or estate, including any or all of the services needed to support it.

Forward Works Programme (FWP), Forward Maintenance Plan (FMP) or Forward Maintenance Register (FMR): A database of works deemed necessary to optimise the performance of a building/estate, or to describe when plant replacement is due to take place, or to satisfy lease, insurance and/or policy mandates.

Hard services/soft services: FM shorthand terms for describing plant and building maintenance and upkeep (hard services), or those relating to supporting the occupants of the building/estate – security, cleaning, catering, couriers and so on (soft services).

Health & Safety or 'H&S': Refers to all Health & Safety legislation, which is prescriptive in its requirements to lessen the risks of harm to persons.

Key Performance Indicators or 'KPIs': A management tool to define performance standards expected of a contractor.

National Audit Office, or 'NAO': The statutorily independent body tasked with overseeing the probity and VFM of government contracts, and to ascertain that public expenditure is in keeping with defined governmental policy of the day.

Office of Government Commerce or 'OGC': An HM Treasury department responsible for best practice in the procurement and management of all public sector contracts (of whatever kind).

Planned Preventative Maintenance or 'PPM': A system for clearly maintaining building plant and fabric to optimise its lifespan, and according to manufacturer's guidelines, insurance requirements and best practice.

Public Accounts Committee, or 'PAC': The remit of the PAC is to examine 'the accounts showing the appropriation of the sums granted by Parliament to meet the public expenditure, and [since 1934] of such other accounts laid before Parliament as the Committee may think fit'.

Service Failure Deductions or 'SFDs': A mechanism to financially penalise a contractor for non-achievement of a service standard or requirement.

Value for Money or 'VFM': 'The optimal use of resources to achieve the intended outcomes' (NAO definition).

Discussion of the Key Concepts Relating To Public Sector Auditing

PERFORMANCE AUDITING

INTOSAI – the International Organisation of Supreme Audit Institutions, an independent international body of public sector audit institutions – has published the following definition of Performance Audit in their paper on Implementation of Performance Auditing: 'Performance auditing is an independent examination of the efficiency and effectiveness of government undertakings, programs or organizations, with due regard to economy, and the aim of leading to improvements.'

Performance auditing, therefore, is concerned with the gamut of public sector let contracts. Performance auditing takes the view that sums are being paid for a service that were competitively let, and notwithstanding that competitive let, must be regularly tested to ensure that:

- the contract is delivering the services expected

- the contract is efficient and effective in doing so

- the contract continues to reflect the public sector requirement, and as it might change throughout the course of that contract's tenure.

This book is a detailed discussion of the subject, as it relates to public sector building/Facilities Management contracts.

INDEPENDENCE

The independence of any auditor commissioned, whether that auditor is an external consultant or any public sector oversight body, is a fundamental tenet of all audit examinations.

Independence in this sense means that an auditor must be left to form his own views based on the audit data presented and discovered without any ability by others to directly influence the content of the report produced. The subject is discussed throughout this book, and where any pre-suppositions and corporate imperatives of the client may contribute to, but will not substantially influence, any audit report.

All those seeking to commission an audit – of whatever type – should continue to hold the view that their auditor's independence is a fundamental cornerstone of a successful audit in itself. An auditor's view will have much more strength if it is unencumbered by specific expectations, and where every aspect of any audit report can be seen to be clear, fair and above board to all parties.

PUBLIC SECTOR VFM/TRANSPARENCY/ACCOUNTABILITY REQUIREMENTS

The public sector has stringent accountability requirements. Funds are devolved to government departments by Parliament, and any budget holder within the public sector has the requirement to ensure that those public funds being spent satisfy all national and EU legislation, and can continually deliver Value For Money.

Key sources of all Treasury requirements for public sector accountability and expenditure management are contained within the 'Green Book', and the 'Orange Book'. The Green Book is 'the central point for access to guidance on the economic assessment of spending and investment and to related guidance including the preparation of business cases for the public sector'. The Orange Book describes 'the concept of risk management and provides a basic introduction to its concepts, development and implementation of risk management processes in government organisations.' These highly technical guidelines provide all public bodies with the tools needed to discharge the roles and funds given to them by Parliament and form key planks of all public sector contractual management.

In practical terms, any government department is accountable to its Accounting Officer, who is then accountable for defending all budget spends to Parliament. The Accounting Officer is normally the permanent head of any Government Department – and therefore part of the Civil Service – and he/she is responsible for overseeing and ensuring the high standards of the organisation he represents.

The major Parliamentary body for overseeing public spend is the Public Accounts Committee (PAC). While the PAC does, in the majority of cases, examine reports made by the National Audit Office (NAO), its powers extend wider than that and the PAC can examine any aspect of public sector expenditure it wishes.

Given that the Accounting Officer is responsible for the ongoing governance, decision-making and financial management of the organisation he represents, and he must make clear statements that the operations and financial probity of the organisation are transparent, clear, free of bias and demonstrate other clear and laudable aims, the Accounting Officer can readily be brought to Parliament to defend his organisational decisions. In practice, this might mean an appearance in front of the PAC, which publishes reports of its examinations.

The HM Treasury publication 'Managing Public Money' sets out the principles for dealing with funds delegated to public sector organisations. Included in the standards expected of an Accounting Officer, and as they relate to this book, are:

- use its resources efficiently, economically and effectively, avoiding waste and extravagance;

- use management information systems to secure assurance about value for money and the quality of delivery and so make timely adjustments;

- use internal and external audit to improve its internal controls and performance.

Ultimately, HM Treasury guidance (in 'Regularity, Propriety and Value for Money') says that if any question remains of a budget holder/Accounting Officer about whether or not funds should be committed/an action taken that results in a business commitment, that two questions should be asked:

- 'Could I satisfactorily defend this before the Public Accounts Committee?'

- 'Since accountability to Parliament is part of a wider accountability, the question might be put even more simply. Could I satisfactorily defend this course of action in public?'

These principles of accountability are referred to throughout the book, and provide a backbone for why the auditing of public sector properties should take place. A diagram on the next page outlines briefly how any funds spent are delegated, and ultimately form part of the democratic process.

The practical truth of public sector accountability is that no civil servant will want to have to justify his departmental expenditure for a service it isn't receiving or isn't receiving to the expected standard, to any of the financial oversight bodies. Public sector accountability, therefore, forms a series of interlocking management arrangements and public sector oversight, all of which are designed to prohibit and inhibit poor management and expenditure.

Every government department and local authority will also have an Internal Audit service/department, whose function is to report to the Accounting Officer on any and all issues found. The Accounting Officer will take formal delivery of an Internal Audit report, and will then be responsible for ensuring that issues found are closed out appropriately. Any department's internal audit service will operate independently, and care is always taken that they remain so. The

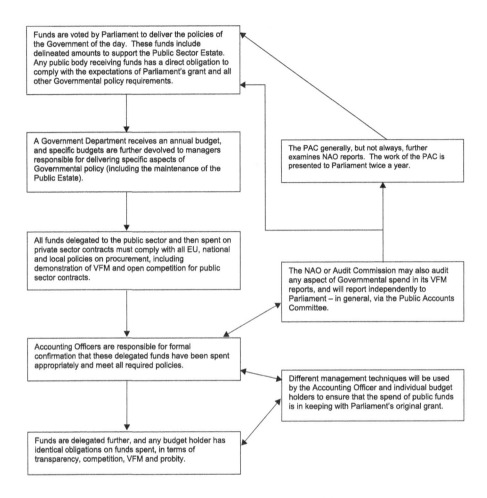

Figure 1.1   Flow-chart of public sector accountability

internal audit service is another mechanism to ensure that careful monitoring does take place of all arrangements, and so to assist the Accounting Officer in his overseeing of his department's expenditure/management. This internal monitoring assists the Accounting Officer in confirming to oversight bodies that public expenditure is in keeping with all policy mandates.

External audit is used as an adjunct to all of these arrangements, and is another useful device for the public sector satisfying its accountability requirements. External audit – the subject of this book – can become part of the public sector's overseeing the workings of any contract or programme, as well as in the auditing of financial statements. External audit reports become public documents like any other, and their opinions remain as part of an internal management tracking of any contract/programme's progress.

Given that public sector accounts are public, it is axiomatic that they must be transparent in themselves. Spend on any FM Contract may be examined by the Accounting Officer/Internal Audit Service/PAC/NAO/ at their leisure, their analysis may be made public and career-changing recommendations made. At issue here is not only what is happening, but what can be seen to be happening. Any and all actions must avoid even the suggestion of impropriety. Any severe criticisms made can have direct detrimental effects on forward budgets (cuts), current and future public sector management (more cuts), and on the contract itself.

This concept of accountability is paramount for the private sector to understand. Letting any public sector contract is only part of a continuum of accountability, and this ongoing understanding of 'is the contract performing as intended' will carry on throughout its tenure. The impact of public sector accountability requirements will be felt in detail for the contract's life.

HARD/SOFT SERVICES, HEALTH & SAFETY/ENVIRONMENTAL SERVICES AND MANAGEMENT REGIMES

Hard services

Hard services are those services that make a building function and relate to engineering and building works. They encompass all engineering tasks, day-to-day maintenance activities, upkeep of any building's fabric and building projects (of whatever kind, though here assumed to be relatively minor) and the management of those services. Hard services require cost-effective compliance with best practice and statutory requirements – adherence to manufacturer's warranties, specialist independent scheduled inspections of some plant by specialist insurers/surveyors (boilers, pressure vessels, lifts, fire equipment and so on) – and most FM Contracts will require any contractor to adhere to all industry guidelines for plant maintenance (CIBSE, HVCA, manufacturers maintenance instructions and so on.)

Generally, hard service management regimes are based on five interdependent requirements as shown on the next page.

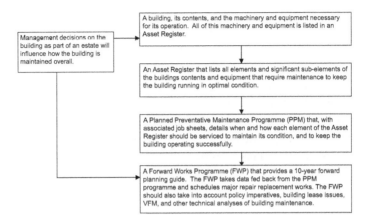

Figure 1.2   Outline of primary hard service management and delivery components

An Asset Register: An Asset Register is, generally, a computer database of all plant to be included in a PPM programme. An Asset Register can be curated many different ways. The choice of curation methodology is a separate subject and is not discussed here. Generally, however, an Asset Register should show clearly which plant must be maintained. The Asset Register will include principal components of that plant (individual sections of a boiler, numbers of different light fittings on a floor by floor basis, and so on). This Asset Register database will automatically produce maintenance requirements, and these requirements become a Planned Preventative Maintenance Programme (PPM).

A Planned Preventative Maintenance programme (PPM): A PPM programme shows a fixed-time list of maintenance activities scheduled to take place having regard to legacy and obsolescence issues. The PPM will set out the requirements for tasks that must be undertaken so as to not invalidate manufacturer's warranties, fulfil all statutory requirements, and to minimise breakdowns/maximise the lifespan of the plant concerned.

A Forward Works Programme (FWP): An FWP is also called a Forward Maintenance Register (FMR) and a Forward Maintenance Programme (FMP) – the titles are interchangeable. An FWP is a considered programme of future works. It is part of a formal asset upgrade and renewal strategy with mission and safety critical drivers based on the asset register and information fed out of the PPM programme. In PPM terms, for example, when an asset can be seen to be at the end of its lifespan, and this is known through regular maintenance checks, a recommendation for plant replacement should automatically be included in the FWP. An FWP is normally constructed to look ahead over 10 years, and should be continually updated to reflect any changes in plant, or changes in estate strategy (that is, a policy decision taken to vacate a building) and any other element. The overall idea of an FWP is to provide building managers with a clear indication of forward costs that become more and more detailed and specific as any new Financial Year approaches.

Soft services

Soft services are those services which relate to anything non-plant: catering, cleaning, restaurant services, security, reception services, post room, reprographics, couriers and so on. Soft services provide the means for building users and visitors to enjoy their building, and to carry out their work without undue concern for safety, cleanliness and with all the amenities contracted for.

Soft services management regimes are based on understanding the timescales for the delivery of any service, and an ongoing understanding of customer contentment with the services provided. Some services – catering, for example – are likely to have contractually-based requirements for delivery of any order within a certain time. Others, like cleaning, are likely to simply require the building to be cleaned to a specified standard for the start of any working day, and with day-cleaners to be on-site for reactive tasks.

Health & safety/environmental services

Health & Safety/Environmental Services sit between hard and soft services and have an impact on each. Health & Safety (H&S) consists of a series of detailed statutory requirements that must be fulfilled (and seen to be fulfilled) in order to lessen the probability of harm to any person in any building concerned. H&S duties are likely to be devolved to some degree to any contractor, but cannot be discharged completely by the public sector (as they remain the client and owner of the building).

The precise point to which any H&S responsibilities can be devolved to a third party is a fine one, and can only be assessed by experts and, ultimately, the courts. In general, however, each individual in any building will have a duty of care so that if anything seen can be considered to be dangerous, or potentially dangerous, that individual has a mandatory duty to report it, and see the issue closed out. A contractor will have a responsibility to ensure that the plant under his care – and including during any maintenance works – does not produce a safety hazard in itself. A public sector manager must regularly check that all is in order – in H&S terms and with due diligence – in the building under his care.

Environmental Services can be undertaken through an FM contractual requirement, or remain inside the public sector. In both instances, the environmental service manager/team will have an ongoing dialogue with their FM contractor to monitor and alter systems to improve a building's environmental performance. Similarly, any contractor-side environmental manager will work closely with public sector managers for any alterations to existing office services – increasing recycling collections, new provisions of more environmentally friendly business products and so on.

FM management regimes for all services are likely to be based on ISO 9001 accreditation, where the contractor has passed fairly stringent ISO requirements for accuracy of documentation. Further, any FM contract is likely to contain requirements for certain types of information to be produced for their client on a regular basis. These requirements can be detailed – a format and content version agreed at time of contract let – or more general – 'to keep an FWP continuously updated and continuously available', for example. FM contract management will also, in terms of transparency, contain a large amount of subsidiary data that is also available to the public sector on an as-needs basis. This information will include items such as training records, all PPM task-sheets, all procurement records, security clearances, staff passes, and so on.

The point about these brief paragraphs on data management is that all service provisions in any public sector contract must be supported by clear management records that will assist the public sector in satisfying their accountability requirements (as above).

HARD AND SOFT DATA

Hard data, to an auditor, is data that is factually based and unequivocal in itself. Hard data is always data that is electronically/paper-based, and so that the data itself can be seen clearly for what it is. Hard data here is, for example, a record showing staff ingress/egress times, signed PPM job sheets, a completed FWP, a list of customer complaints. Hard data is not anecdotal.

Soft data is data that cannot be seen to be true and clear. Soft data is data that is ambiguous, or incomplete. Auditors will consider data to be soft if it cannot be seen to be part of a contractual construct (as in, if it is an isolated piece of information without any tangible use), or where, by testing, the data can be seen to be unworkable or meaningless to some degree or another. An example here might be when a Helpdesk call can be manipulated on the system itself as to the time the call occurred, and when any action did take place. An auditor will consider that datum to be potentially 'soft' because the actions cannot be seen to be clearly true and unable to be manipulated. Soft data can also be personal opinions as to an aspect of the contract, where the opinion was found to be interesting but impossible to prove one way or another.

REDRESS

Webster's English Dictionary defines 'redress' as 'to set right; rectify or remedy, often by making compensation for (a wrong, grievance, and so on)'.

Redress, in practical audit-related terms, can mean one of two things:

- To force improvement according to contract, and by recourse to law if necessary;

- To seek financial compensation for failures.

Audit is an effective tool to support any public sector body looking for either of the above two results. An audit, if it is well founded, can provide a completely transparent mechanism for ensuring that everyone can understand the detail of any failure (and so the potential for any kind of redress).

STATUTORY REQUIREMENTS

Statutory requirements are legislation that demands specific actions. Statutory requirements, in relation to building/FM auditing, tend to concentrate on Health & Safety legislation and, within that, on those elements of building maintenance that can most dramatically affect the well-being of building users. Examples of this might be: testing for legionella contamination, lift maintenance, safety of pressure vessels, power supply, COSHH registers.

The auditing of statutory requirements are a clear and concise subject area for any auditor to examine. While this book does not discuss the immensely complex areas of H&S legislation, we might note that an effective audit of any FM Contractor's H&S compliance will assist in discharging the public sector's 'duty of care'.

MICRO/MACRO EXAMINATIONS AND VERTICAL/HORIZONTAL AUDITING

Micro/macro and horizontal/vertical auditing are two similar audit techniques that assist in understanding any individual piece of evidence within any context, or to look at the broad functioning of a contract overall.

Micro/macro audit examinations are those that take a single piece of audit data (a training record, for example) and place that single piece of data in its context within the contract. This training record would then be seen for the data it is (complete/incomplete) but also within the context of training requirements as a whole. This one record would ultimately assist in informing the auditors opinions on the success or otherwise of the contract as a whole.

Conversely, a macro examination would show if staff training did largely fulfil the training requirements as a whole through sampling of pan-contract training records. A macro examination would look across the breadth of the training requirements within the contract, and form opinions through sampling if the area was compliant/non-compliant with the contractual requirement for training of site staff.

Vertical/horizontal audit examinations are those that either:

- Take an overall subject matter and examine its compliance through the strata of management records and compliance requirements to a single piece of evidence, and back to the overall requirement again to ascertain its place within the contractual requirement as a whole, and thus to understand if the requirement is being fulfilled from its detail to the overall intent of the requirement.

- Look at a contract or a contractual obligation in its breadth, to determine its compliance within the extent of the service/stream obligations as a whole.

- Using the example above, a vertical examination of training would understand that appropriate training of site staff did continuously take place, and follow management procedures and practices down to specific staff training records. A horizontal examination of training would include training obligations within the context of overall contractual requirements as a whole.

2

The Need for Performance Auditing

'I wouldn't lie to you! What would be the point of that?'
An FM Contract Manager

Introduction

If one accepts that knowledge is power, a performance auditing regime can bring a wealth of power to public sector property managers. If any manager is truly interested in understanding if his public sector budget is being spent properly, and so to avoid any criticism by the Accounting Officer, National Audit Office, or (ultimately) the Public Accounts Committee, it behoves that manager to know that he is receiving what he has paid for, and to the standard expected.

Ensuring that the performance standard is as expected is as important as any other aspect of building management. Achieving a required standard, for the private sector, involves a greater or lesser expenditure of corporate financial and personnel commitment dependent on any specific service area. Therefore, for a public body to accept that performance can be less than contractually required, is to give the private sector an unexpected financial bonus (because the private sector can spend less on delivering the service, and keep the amount originally budgeted).

If a contract was well let, with a robust tendering and competitive exercise, any contractor should have priced their bid to achieve exactly the service level described and with a reasonable overhead and profit element. If, through oversight and negligence, these standards are not continuously required, contractors might consider it foolish not to claw some expenditure back, and so to improve their profitability.

Audits are multi-disciplinary and can be undertaken in a myriad of different ways, and by either the public or private sectors. An audit can be a sample check of soft services adequacy on an occasional basis by a client-side FM manager, or a formal annual review by a bespoke consultancy. An audit can be forensic, to discover fraud or practices that contravene statute, or almost collaborative with the contractor, in order to assist in a partnering sense with performance improvement. An Audit can last over minutes, or months.

While this book is meant to be a guideline for public sector FM managers to assist in their commissioning of any kind of audit, it is also meant to be an argument for any kind of a considered audit programme, by whichever body. The idea of a considered audit is for the client/public sector manager to think clearly about 'what it is he wishes to understand', and to develop a systematic way of understanding that issue. The issue can be overall performance, or financial probity. It can be security services, or Health & Safety compliance, or any single element or combination of elements that comprise an FM contract.

Performance audits are pieces of string – they can be as long or as short as one likes, and the issue(s) under consideration, as well as any number of contributory factors, will influence their construction, timing and potential for positive change.

In truth, there is really no right or wrong in any audit a public sector property manager might choose to undertake, by whatever means, provided it is independent and factually based. Undertaking a one-off audit has a different value to a rolling audit, and a choice to do one or the other will depend on the circumstances of any FM contract at the time, and its place within the public sector manager's overall responsibilities. A major mistake in public sector building management regime would be not to audit.

This chapter describes some of the overarching positives of a performance audit:

- three types of audit programmes

- transparency of any contract's progress

- the potential financial ramifications of a performance audit

- positive change for the public and private sectors.

Together, these four sections set the stage for a more detailed discussion of the audit process. They provide the groundwork for an understanding of what a performance audit/audit regime might do for any manager looking to commission one.

Three Types of Audit Programmes

In terms of audit construction, there are three main audit strategies that can be considered in forming a decision on any issue in question. While audit constructs become substantially more detailed, as discussed below, these three basic forms of an audit are the first point of decision for a client management team:

A One-Off Audit: For understanding any subject in detail.

A rolling programme of audits: For understanding and testing any contract overall over a period of time, and so to confirm progress made.

Spot Checks: For receiving an immediate confirmation that any subject is largely in order or not.

Obviously, property performance audits will answer specific questions of concern to the client team. Specific questions, however, can be about the health of the contract overall rather than a simple examination of a single service stream. Broadly based contract health checks in a one-off audit will examine all contractual provisions, including management regimes, procurement processes, and on-site delivery. On a micro level, confirmation can be requested from an auditor on specific technical subjects (eg that statutory inspections and maintenance are taking place as mandated, or that a contractor's Health & Safety policies are up-to-date and appropriate).

ONE-OFF AUDITS

One-off audits can be useful. One-off audits tend to be undertaken to answer a specific question in some detail, and where ongoing compliance requirements are tested elsewhere in different ways. One-off audits can be used to verify results given by others, or to form an initial opinion as to the necessity for any greater management input – pursuit of fraud or a major management non-compliance, for example. The point here, however, is that a one-off audit can provide meaningful data that can provide the mechanism for clarity and/or change. Because a one-off audit is likely to be structured to gain a detailed understanding of the subject, it can be used to drive detailed change on a subject felt to be failing or to provide a broad assurance that all is in order.

ROLLING AUDIT PROGRAMME

Performance audits can also be undertaken on a rolling basis, to regularly deliver a comment on the state of play and compliance of the contractual provisions overall. A considered strategy of regular audits – annually, biannually or quarterly – can provide regular independent benchmarkable assessments. A rolling programme will tell the client whether a contract is performing well over time, if issues recur, or if any change management programmes are achieving the results expected. There is no right or wrong strategy here either, and the choice of frequency of any audit programme will always depend on the perceived success of their contract at any one time, local policies and individual management strategies.

SPOT CHECKS

Spot checks, based on a percentage of performance requirements (deliverables) can give a realistic picture of how a contract is performing, by applying a percentage success/failure rate across a contractual provision, from the success/failure ratio found during the sample. Given that it is never possible to examine 100 per cent of any service delivery at any point during any contract, all audits will be based on the audit practice of extrapolating meaningful data from a relevant sample. This, in itself can be undertaken in different ways.

For example, a spot check can also be undertaken in real time. We were once requested to walk with a client and his contractor through a building, and to make an assessment of Health & Safety compliance/non-compliance found. Here, the client was able to see what the audit expert saw, and ask him why his oral opinions were as they were. This H&S spot check produced a 'checklist' report, which provided a very succinct summary of the sample-based audit.

A spot-check of records would mean, to an auditor, examining a representative number of records/activities in order to draw more general conclusions. Records drawn would be random, and based on normal assessments of proportionality. For example: if any service stream had 500 individual outputs in any one month, or some 6,000 per annum, a representative sampling would be in the region of 10 per cent of any month, or (say) 5 per cent of the annual output. The sampling needs to be wide enough to be able to compare results, but not so wide as to be disproportionate to the exercise. The subject of statistical sampling is discussed further elsewhere in this book.

TO SUMMARISE

Audit data can be useful to both parties considering or facing an audit. One-off audit data can tell client side management if their own perception of contractor performance is (more or less) accurate, or not. On the contractor side, a one-off audit can allow them to see if, corporately, they are at risk of not delivering their core requirements.

While a case-study on a long-term audit strategy follows at the conclusion of this book, we would just note here that a reasonable long-term strategy allows for trend analysis and to be able to assess, realistically, if one's contractor is improving or worsening over time. This information can directly benefit future client decisions (a future procurement exercise, for example).

A spot check at any point can provide an almost instantaneous overview of any subject. A spot check can be used to provide immediate confirmation on a subject, or an indicative view of compliance/non-compliance on any subject, or range of subjects.

An audit is worth nothing if not acted upon by both the contractor and the client. Change should be a direct result of any audit undertaken.

Transparency and Financial Ramifications

TRANSPARENCY

Transparency, for an auditor, is to be able to see clearly – from start to finish – the detailed workings of a process, a task, a project or a contract. Transparency also means that management implications of any subject being considered are similarly open and able to be understood. Transparency is oft-quoted by auditors in a negative sense: 'insufficient transparency of process exists', 'there is a lack of transparency as to a project's procurement', and so on. Transparency is one of the key concepts that any auditor works towards – if a process/task/ project/contract is fully transparent, and that transparency shows foundation mechanisms that are accurate, appropriate and compliant, and with little or no likelihood of being open to individual manipulation then any auditor is going to be content (in that sense).

In terms of the audit process assisting the public sector, knowing if a subject area is or is not transparent helps the discharge of financial accountability obligations. Understanding any process in detail will show the likelihood of any inappropriate private sector management actions, and will therefore allow the public sector to take remedial action quickly if failure exists.

Pragmatically, in a financial sense, insisting on transparency of processes reduces the potential for fraud and wastage of public sector funds. While contractors are particularly sensitive about financial data concerning revenue and profit, and this is understandable, any legitimate demand for sight of it cannot be reasonably refused.

Transparency is one of the terms most capable of being misunderstood by those being audited. We have had it interpreted as an attempt by ourselves to look at inappropriate commercially confidential subjects, as attempting to look far beyond what we might need to establish to confirm any individual contract compliance/performance point, and to look at all records held by the contractor just for interest's sake. If this brief paragraph is preaching to a contractor – we'd like to emphasise that no auditor will consider any examination complete until he fully understands the process of the subject under consideration, and any attempt to limit that understanding will be treated as a management flaw in itself.

There are two other polar-opposite strategies we've come across in the guise of resisting the provision of appropriate data to understand a process (resisting transparency):

- A contractor who decided if he didn't show anything, or not very much, that we couldn't conduct the audit (and therefore he couldn't fail). He failed.

- A contractor who decided to bury us in detail, so we would have no hope in separating out what was of interest. We found what we were looking for.

Both strategies are borderline bad faith, and should be treated as such. Any auditor here would make the direct observation that the audit was limited, stymied or needlessly complicated through management intransigence, and recommend that a further examination to uncover what the contractor tried to hide, using any contractual mechanism necessary to do so, should occur at the earliest possible opportunity.

More positively and practically, a transparent process would work something like the examples below. We are using an example of a Planned Preventative Maintenance programme in depth, to show how we would understand if the PPM schedules were robust and that PPM was taking place as scheduled. Ultimately, this analysis would show if PPM processes were transparent, or not. To assist, the diagram below sets out how a PPM process works overall.

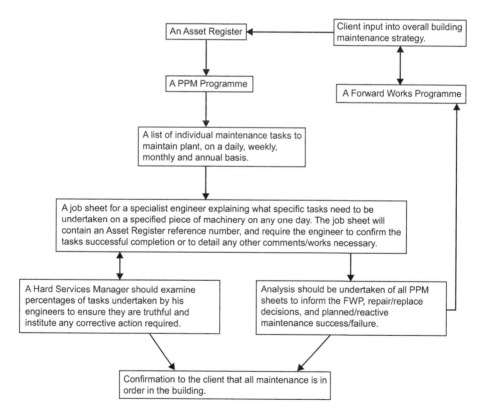

Figure 2.1   Outline of the PPM management process

To understand, therefore, if the PPM programme is working according to industry standards and applicable legislation, these are the types of questions that would be asked:

- What is the construct of the building's asset register, and how/how often is it updated?

- What is the management protocol informing when changes to the asset register require a change to the PPM schedule, and do we agree with the protocol?

- How is the PPM schedule updated – in terms of regularity and guaranteed adherence to the agreed asset register strategy?

- What happens with a PPM job-sheet? Whom does it go to, and does it contain all necessary information?

- Have the jobs been carried out as specified? What supervisory checks have been made on implementation? Is PPM fully integrated with the asset renewal and upkeep strategy expressed in the Forward Works Programme? Are items excluded from PPM which should be incorporated within it?

- How are returned PPM sheets treated? What management decisions inform any updating on any PPM system, or asset register? Who checks, and how, that PPM checks are actually being undertaken as scheduled?

The answers to these questions would show us if there were clear linkages between process and the practical exercise of plant maintenance itself. There are technical details that inform PPM programmes. We would look for a seamless marriage of elements in building maintenance that inform any PPM programme, as all elements have a distinct and important role to play in its contractual fulfilment. We would look to see rational and current management consideration being made of these technically complex issues, and to see those reflected in the raw data itself.

To illustrate: we knew of a contractor whose PPM programme appeared to be working well, and we were asked to verify if this perception was true. In our audit we had sundry questions about various technical issues, but the major failing we saw was that the worksheets filled out by any engineer undertaking a PPM task were never examined or used to influence the Asset Register or Forward Works Programme. The failure to take note of what an engineer had discovered, or done, during a routine maintenance task was a fairly serious management fault, and meant that PPM itself was being undertaken in a kind of isolated void as any changes to the plant being maintained were not being reflected elsewhere.

The engineer's input into what he physically saw and did during his plant visit was a central part of the PPM programme. Without his input, PPM would simply roll on in its tracks – which it was – but with no real management knowledge of whether or not what he said was accurate, or if PPM was becoming disproportionate having regard to the lifespan of the plant (and therefore should be some provision incorporated within the FWP), or whether or not the Asset Register should be updated (because of a significant component replacement).

Going back to our list of questions above, if we found the PPM programme to be robust here, we could provide reasonable assurance that the building's plant was being maintained properly. This would mean that the client could forward-budget with more confidence, as he should not expect major surprises in terms of unscheduled plant replacement.

If we found that PPM was not being managed well, and this could be in any manner of ways, and to greater or lesser extents, we would inform the client of a likelihood of unforeseen expenditure at some point. The lack of clarity surrounding plant maintenance would mean a lack of certainty regarding plant condition – and therefore the ongoing budgets necessary to repair/replace.

While the above scenario would provide a solid basis for immediate to mid-term financial liabilities – as the client would know to a reasonable degree that expensive elements of plant were being maintained properly, and proper warning of obsolescence is likely to be given – probing further would provide more detailed assurance.

If we were to look a bit further into transparency of the process we would attempt to take the issue full circle into high-level long-term management implications of the process and look to understand:

- How is any PPM data analysed? Who makes a decision, and how, based on the correlation between PPM maintenance and reactive works, if any item of plant is due for replacement rather than continuous repair? How is the decision justified?

- Who monitors the correlation between planned and reactive tasks in their proper context? Does the contractor have a view on reactive/ planned weighting over the lifespan of plant, and is that view used to inform their clients as to future works?

- Is PPM cost effective in itself? Can its benefits be quantified?

- How are PPM results communicated to the client? Does the information presented tell them what they need to know to make informed budgetary decisions?

The answers to these questions would allow for assurance or non-assurance of the accuracy of mid-long-term financial planning. If the answers to the questions were largely positive, the client could have reasonable certainty of few budgetary surprises as the condition of the plant can be seen to be understood in detail. If the answers were negative, we would indicate that forward budgeting could only be guesstimates to a greater or lesser degree.

FINANCIAL RAMIFICATIONS

A problem for any contractor, especially in a PFI Contract, is that transparency of processes may well result in financial penalties. The question can be, for a contractor, 'How do I appear to be cooperative, while doing everything I can to hide results I don't wish to be seen?' To be fair here, there is no doubt that some contractors have been successfully beating an audit from time immemorial.

The point should be made, though, that auditors tend to question more closely any contractor who is in any way economical with the truth. As financial penalties will only ever be levied on the basis of known and demonstrable facts, seeing a contractor trying their best to deflect a reasonable question will only make any auditor more curious and more determined to find what is being hidden, and the reason for such attempts to be made. One contractor we've known over the years has a practice of only answering very specifically the exact question put to him and ignore any other inferences contained in the question. While we might smile, any auditor would have no problem with that practice. Contractors, however, who promise that a document is at hand, but has mysteriously gone missing, will be treated with some scepticism after a short period of time.

Auditors will take the view that a bona fide contract was entered into, in which a contractor will have priced for risk, and the level of compliance and performance contained within the agreement. If a contractor wilfully obfuscates with a vague hope that the process will eventually grind to a halt, the only result is likely to be the auditor recommending that their own costs be recovered (along with any penalties for any service default).

Of course, increasingly, the idea of service failures will likely come down to financial redress as opposed to instigating management mechanisms for simply improving performance faults.

Service Failure Deductions (SFDs), or provisions allowing the public sector to recoup sums through other means in the event of breakdowns in service, were and are constructed to provide a financial incentive to help concentrate the private sector's mind on keeping performance at a high level. The idea here, cynical and truthful, is that having the ability to take profit away from the private sector (whether or not that ability is ever exercised) is the only certain way to make them perform to contractual expectations.

The imposition of financial penalties will always be governed by a degree of discretion. Our experience is that contractors both rely on that, and forget it (at the same time). In general, the public sector is more interested in seeing constant good faith effort over time, rather than insisting on swingeing financial penalties with every chance that they get. While the above statements are sweeping generalities, the premises are borne out by government good practice.

Good practice means leaving the contractor to do his job, provided he acts in good faith and according to the requirements set out in the contract. Private sector corporate imperatives means that protecting profit levels is equally important to satisfying their contractual obligations to the letter.

Treasury guidance bears out the concept of promoting performance as equal to insisting on financial penalties. VFM is seen as an insistence on quality as well as achieving a strong commercial price through competition. The National Audit Office definition of VFM quoted above as – 'the optimal use of resources to achieve the intended outcomes' – neatly summarises the balancing act that VFM is meant to achieve. Quality (the intended outcome is a quality product/service) must be an equal driving force with cost. Expending significant management or consultant time to seek financial redress could be disproportionate ('a non optimal use of resources') if the problem isn't serious enough, or the risk of not achieving the desired outcome (improvement/ financial redress) is high.

However, and given that all budget holders in the public sector are ultimately accountable to Parliament, not seeking financial redress for a known deficiency or because of fraud, is to waste public sector funds and to misuse public sector trust. If VFM is a bedrock of public sector procurement, and where VFM should be tested throughout a contract, seeking redress when any exploitation of public funds is occurring must be a corollary of the concept.

For the private sector then, our feeling is that a pervasive miasma of fear exists where the contractor is all-too-clear where financial penalties might reasonably be imposed and thus potentially driving a knee-jerk 'we must hide' attitude. This knowledge of the true corporate effects of any financial penalties on profit levels or contract sum is combined with a (reasonably justified) assurance that the public sector may not insist on their being levied.

An auditor will leave such decisions in their client's hands – it is, generally, a step too far for an auditor to opine on this strategic corporate level. In that sense, an auditor's results should speak for themselves, and provide a reasonable assessment framework as to whether a financial penalty is justified or not. This assessment would be dependent on the degree and pervasiveness of non-compliance or non-performance with the contract. Again, it is a mistake of the private sector to believe that an auditor is attending simply to seek financial redress. An auditor's job is to consider performance carefully, and opine carefully, on what is found.

Playing it differently, though, the public sector should be able to rely on any performance auditor's report to seek financial redress if they so desire. Any auditor, obviously, will know the contract concerned intimately, will be cognisant of the financial ramifications of opinions expressed and can calculate them if requested. The benefit of a proper audit, properly briefed and executed, is that the findings will withstand any enquiry and thus lead to financial recompense if and when desired.

Positive Change

The public sector should always request their auditor to summarise any audit into a list of desirable actions. In its most formal sense these recommendations become a change management plan, which is formally agreed by the contractor. Audits, while providing much interesting data for those who care to analyse it, are best used if they can assist change in day-to-day activities that can be seen by management and end-users.

A change management process resulting from audit is a useful tool in assisting the public sector to satisfy its accountability requirements. For the public sector, being able to continuously demonstrate that strong positive steps are being taken to confirm the contract's performance and management will provide some reassurance to concerned others that the contract's management is in order. A formal or informal change management procedure supports contract management in demonstrating that any contract is being run properly.

Recommendations made in an audit can be used formally, or informally. Used formally, audit recommendations form part of the client's management strategy (in terms of tracking performance progress) and can – if desired – form part of the next formal audit. Used informally, audit recommendations allow for an ongoing dialogue to take place between contractor and client – to provide a kind of touchstone as to how recommendations might be bedding in.

In a mid-long-term audit programme, it can be of great benefit to track change over time. In this type of an audit programme, the auditor would look back at the previous audit, and with its agreed recommendations, to assess if the change has been implemented (and implemented well) and comment on the effectiveness of changes as part of the next audit report. The benefit of such a strategy is obvious, of course – over time, the client-side management team will have a clear story to tell of progress made, and where performance can be clearly tracked over time.

In a one-off audit, which may be looking in more detail at one particular subject, changes recommended can be as detailed as the subject matter requires, and the expectation will be that any change management programme will be overseen by the client management team.

In an audit some years ago, we were concerned that some management information wasn't being incorporated fully into a contractor's Quality

Management system. Our observation was (in effect) that: 'We recommend that training records are continuously updated, so that they can be proved to be accurate, and so that the contractor can demonstrate clearly to his client that all site staff are trained appropriately for their role.'

The action plan in this case broke down the audit point into three subsidiary steps – ascertain what training had demonstrably been given, close any gaps in training required for individual roles, and construct an up-to-date training matrix showing the present and future training programme – with deadlines for implementation. Given that the contractor, after completion, would be making unambiguous statements on the subject, the client management team could readily and easily check compliance and performance with the (accepted) recommendation to only have on site personnel appropriately qualified for their role.

Given the contractor's acceptance of the recommendation, if further inaccurate statements were seen to be wilfully inaccurate, any subsequent audit would take a firmer view on the failing (that is, consider it to be significant, because of presenting something as 'true' when it was demonstrably 'false').

The private sector has – for all obvious reasons to do with the audit process – generally refused to see an audit as a potentially positive management tool. A contractor who understands the benefits of an audit can allow for change that is not forced, and allow for a greater openness in all client-side discussions of any performance faults.

While no auditor will tell any contractor specifically how to run their business in great detail, all auditors will be content to provide enough of a road map to a contractor about how to become compliant on the subject according to their specific contract, and all public sector policy imperatives. Government guidance requires specific skills for quantitative analysis in areas such as risk, investment appraisal, tender analysis, statistical methodology, project controls and so on. The auditor will often benchmark the contractor's performance on the presumption of particular skills being applied when appropriate.

In some ways, for an auditor, recommending detailed change can walk a fairly fine line between sketching the way forward and drawing up a detailed blueprint for how the service should be performed. The amount of detail any auditor might feel advisable to include will vary, dependent on the subject under consideration.

FOR EXAMPLE:

If small works procurement, which has been delegated to a contractor, it will be subject to HM Treasury and local policies on procurement. If the procurement is found to be not fully transparent, or faulty in any other way, an auditor will feel there to be no harm in reminding the contractor of contractual requirements, and public sector procurement imperatives.

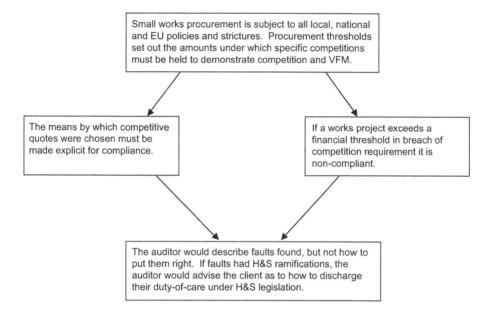

Figure 2.2   Example of auditor input into small works procurement fault

If a management system is flawed and so that the contract cannot be seen to be running under a robust quality management system, an auditor is likely to simply recommend that the system changes. An auditor, here, will feel that the contractor should be able to see the problem clearly in itself, having regard to the appropriate skill-sets, and integrate any changes perfectly within his broader management regime.

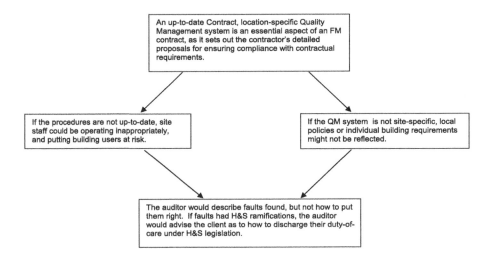

Figure 2.3   Example of auditor input into quality management systems

If Health & Safety records are incomplete, an auditor is likely to strongly advise immediate change, and remind the contractor of his statutory obligations by citation of appropriate regulations. The auditor, however, will not tell the contractor chapter and verse of Health & Safety legislation, or how to integrate any changes within his management regime as a whole. To do so would

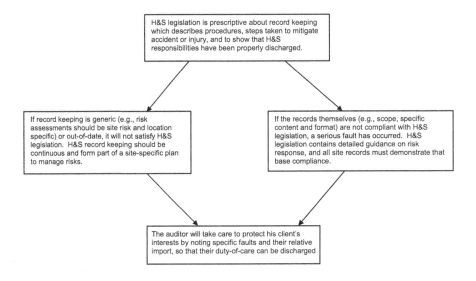

Figure 2.4   Example of auditor input into health & safety issues

demand a disproportionate amount of auditor time, and would effectively provide a contractor with expertise that should already be in place.

There are exceptions of course, and some examples are contained elsewhere in this book. If a contract is working perfectly in a partnering sense, it is possible for an auditor to be instructed to work closely with the contractor to see that any changes made will satisfy the auditor.

Here, an auditor effectively becomes a good practice guide, and provides any and all information necessary to assist the contractor in becoming compliant on the subject concerned. This strategy is wholly healthy. Any auditor will always be able to understand the subject they have opined upon in detail, and so can be a valuable resource to the FM management team as a whole. For the client team, knowing that their auditor is working with their contractor to improve the area under consideration simply means that performance will be improved and be seen clearly to be so. There is no conflict of interest, as the auditor's client remains the public sector, whose desire is to see demonstrable rapid improvement.

Whatever the audit programme, or whatever the subject matter, good practice says that any changes recommended in any audit report should be formally agreed with the contractor concerned. An auditor will generally recommend that the contractor clearly accepts recommendations made in any report, and so becomes corporately committed to improvement.

This discussion and negotiation of recommended changes is an important adjunct to a successful audit change management programme. Having a contractor understand the reasons for recommended changes, and giving that contractor the ability to challenge them and/or understand the background in more detail, provides more buy-in to the process and ultimately makes the change management programme more transparent in itself.

The other side of the coin is that of forced step-change improvement. Here, and this is also perfectly legitimate, any client can simply present their contractor with a list of actions to be taken, and require the contractor to complete them by a certain date. The advantages of this approach – minimising management time, demonstrating a strong corporate will – are clear-cut. In this instance, the client management team shows their contractor that they are confident of the actions to be made, and simply require the contractor to work out how changes must be made.

The choice of whether to seek contractor buy-in to a change management programme, or to force that process, or to informally agree an informal process is heavily dependent on the state of the contract and contractor/client relations at the time. If a contractor is continually intransigent about corporate change, there is likely to be no real advantage in entering into a long debate about the minutiae of further steps that need to be taken. If the contractor/client relationship is strong, and working in a partnering sense, incorporating a change management plan into ongoing management dialogue simply becomes an adjunct to the process.

Summary

A long-term audit programme can (and perhaps should) have a change management programme that operates in parallel with the audits. As any new audit takes place, the audit team looks at previous reports to satisfy themselves that acceptable changes have taken place on the previous subject matters, and opines both on changes, and the new subject areas. The strategy allows for mid-long-term description of improvements made. A long-term performance audit programme is ultimately of most value for the public sector.

A one-off audit will tend to look at more detail, and where an auditor will recommend changes to the degree appropriate to the subject matter, but without providing the contractor with all minute management steps that should likely be made. A one-off audit will assume that the client-side management team will oversee any changes made, and will not concern itself with how.

A spot check can provide immediate feedback on any issue, in real time or as a relatively brief look at any subject(s) of concern. A spot check is meant to be time-limited for the auditor, and is distinct from a one-off audit because of that. A spot check can provide a good, realistic, assessment of the likelihood of strong compliance/non-compliance, but without a detailed examination of any underpinnings of any fault found.

Having formal contractor buy-in to any changes recommended is a matter of good practice, and provides for less ongoing management time in debating whether or not the changes were/are truly necessary. If a contractor is allowed to discuss/dispute/negotiate changes recommended before final publication of a report, the client management team have the certainty of knowing that their contractor is formally and corporately committed to the process. The contractor can, therefore, be challenged formally if no progress is subsequently made.

An audit programme can also help the client management team further understand if their own arrangements are working well. In general, this understanding comes through exceptions in an audit report – if repeated observations are made that an action hasn't been accomplished due to lack of client decision-making, the inferences to be drawn are fairly clear. Of course, audits can also be commissioned by any client to look at if client support of the contract is working as intended, in parallel with the examination of FM subjects.

Financial redress in case of serious failure should be sought. Many current contracts are let with an FM contractor pricing a degree of risk, and that risk includes the risk of failure in service delivery. This book does not go into a detailed discussion of the management decisions that need to be made to pursue financial redress from any failing contractor. The point we make here is that a properly constructed performance audit can also be the foundation for pursuit of monies.

3

Four Basic Audit Constructs

'We can do this easy, or we can do this hard – it's up to you.'
American saying

Introduction

This chapter looks at the broad overall types of property performance audits. Distinctions between the types of audit approaches identified is somewhat artificial, as most audit approaches contain different elements of each, and use a myriad of different techniques to understand the audit question posed.

An audit approach is the superstructure of any audit being considered. Concepts are interrelated. Even if contractor/client relations are excellent and being conducted in a partnering sense, contractor systems could be sufficiently out-of-date so as to conceal impropriety and so demand a toughening of those relationships until corrective action has taken place. A straightforward performance audit is likely to contain elements of cooperation with the contractor, as well as a deep vertical examination of one or more subjects.

For a property manager planning to commit to an audit, or an audit regime, knowing that the different audit approaches assist in defining what might be discovered, is a useful starting point for probing the subjects in more detail.

The four basic audit construct types are:

- a straightforward performance/compliance audit

- a forensic audit, or a contentious audit

- a partnering audit

- a modular audit.

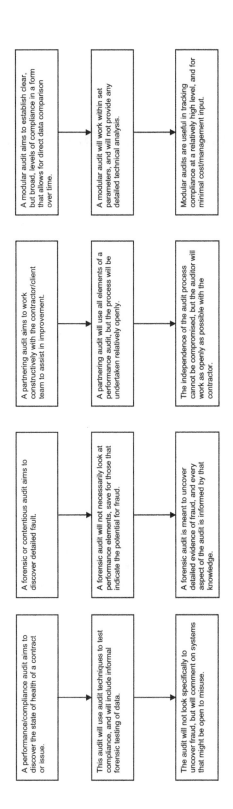

Figure 3.1   Broad overview of four different audit constructs

A performance/compliance audit aims to discover the state of health of a contract or issue.

This audit will use audit techniques to test compliance, and will include informal forensic testing of data.

The audit will not look specifically to uncover fraud, but will comment on systems that might be open to misuse.

A forensic or contentious audit aims to discover detailed fault.

A forensic audit will not necessarily look at performance elements, save for those that indicate the potential for fraud.

A forensic audit is meant to uncover detailed evidence of fraud, and every aspect of the audit is informed by that knowledge.

A partnering audit aims to work constructively with the contractor/client team to assist in improvement.

A partnering audit will use all elements of a performance audit, but the process will be undertaken relatively openly.

The independence of the audit process cannot be compromised, but the auditor will work as openly as possible with the contractor.

A modular audit aims to establish clear, but broad, levels of compliance in a form that allows for direct data comparison over time.

A modular audit will work within set parameters, and will not provide any detailed technical analysis.

Modular audits are useful in tracking compliance at a relatively high level, and for minimal cost/management input.

These audit constructs are discussed in detail in this chapter, and can be outlined diagrammatically opposite:

A Performance or Compliance Audit

A performance audit is more straightforward than others. Its overall intention is to confirm that the FM house is in order, and to tease out any areas that could be improved. A performance audit doesn't anticipate probing the detail of management strategies, VFM confirmation, KPI examination, or procurement, although it will examine the subjects sufficiently to understand if all is generally in order. This audit might make recommendations for further studies if any details of non-compliance are found to be serious and will contain an action list.

A straightforward performance audit also assumes a lack of obstruction and with clear client objectives. This audit approach also infers a clear distinction between client and contractor, where their relations are formal and constructive. This audit structure assumes that a clear audit report is desired, where the contractor will be informed of its results in due course, and is distinct from a 'partnering audit' where the contractor becomes more involved in the process itself (with limitations).

A performance audit is simply what it says on the tin. It aims to examine if the contract is functioning well, and according to its contractual obligations. Performance audits only get complicated because of the breadth of subjects that are normally covered in any building/property audit, and because of the techniques used to assess performance properly.

This section, and the others looking at other broad audit types, outlines more of the differentiations between them, and so to provide an overview of factors that influence their choice and execution.

A HYPOTHETICAL EXAMPLE OF WHERE A STRAIGHTFORWARD PERFORMANCE AUDIT SHOULD BE COMMISSIONED

An FM Manager, client-side, wakes up one day and decides that a performance audit on the functioning of his property is just the ticket. The client knows that he has kept a light touch overview on how his FM Contractor has been managing, and he knows that incidents of complaints – though vehement when they come – are around minor issues, and he largely understands the reasons for failure. However, the FM Contract is approaching an anniversary date, and he knows that a request for further funding is likely to come his way from his contractor. The client-side FM manager ponders a bit, and decides that double-checking levels of compliance might help him managerially and financially in the short-mid-term future.

An external auditor is duly appointed and is given a brief like this:

- We wish to confirm compliance/performance with our FM Contract across hard and soft services, and Health & Safety.

- We have fairly good relations with our contractor, and have no overall problems with his performance.

- We have three buildings in South East England, with a combined occupancy of 4,000 people. The contract covers all services.

- The contract has not been formally audited before, although in-house client-side checks have been made with some regularity.

- We want the audit to be comprehensive – in terms of looking at all aspects of compliance/performance – but we don't anticipate it being forensic (that is, we don't anticipate that any inappropriate or fraudulent actions are taking place).

- We wish, ultimately, for formal assurance to be given to us that all is generally in order, or to identify areas where improvements should take place.

- We expect to use the audit results as a mechanism for future discussions with the contractor, and so expect it to be sufficiently specific to provide us with enough information to inform any future variations/uplifts.

- We have no real opinion as to timing, but would like a draft report within the next two months.

In terms of preparation, the auditor would then:

- Prepare a more detailed brief for formal agreement by his client. This brief would also include details of the audit team, timescale, client-side involvement required, timing (of the audit itself and the report) and a budget.

- The auditor will suggest dates for the audit, and likely recommend that a formal pre-briefing takes place where the client informs his contractor of the audit's commissioning.

- The auditor will take his agreed brief, and break it down further, as below. At this point, client-side agreement becomes unnecessary, and the new document will provide a detailed working guide for the audit team.

- At that point, the auditor will likely prepare a separate list of documentation required, and present it to the contractor formally. General practice is to present this information-requested-list a reasonable time before the audit is to take place.

In terms of the audit itself, the audit team would know:

- The contractor is unlikely to be seriously obstructive, as the process will be new to them in this contract. This means that no extensive time needs to be built in for arguments with the contractor about the process itself, and where the terms of reference should suffice to commence the process.

- The three buildings in a discrete geographical territory also means that the workings of all three can be sampled, and the audit constructed so that all buildings can be looked at on site (as well as the overarching management structures).

- The overall health check means that sampling should occur across all service areas, and the audit team commissioned accordingly. Given that the audit is a new one for the contract, the audit would likely be constructed to look at an even representation of management structures/site delivery.

- Given that the client manager is looking for an overall assurance as to performance, or specific areas where improvement might be made, the audit team will be instructed to think laterally about any subject examined. Any management recommendations made that are not service specific would need to be verified to confirm their direct impact on service provision.

- The audit would expect to last 4–5 days, with a team of four (including the audit leader), and with a draft report available within three weeks after conclusion of the audit.

To summarise, performance audits – and again this is a fairly broad statement – are meant to look at relatively straightforward levels of compliance/performance against contractual requirements (the service specification). They are meant to provide assurance (somewhat qualified, of necessity) that all is generally in order. The audit will specify any overall areas of concern that should be held by the public sector and/or the FM Contractor.

Undertaking a broad performance/compliance audit is of use to both client and contractor, and provides the fastest way of understanding if the contract is broadly on course. This construct means that the contractor understands that he is subject to audit, and is prepared to cooperate. In turn, this means that the performance auditor can concentrate on his assessment in the relative security of knowing that he is likely to be given all that he asks for without undue delay.

On the public sector's side, knowing that this audit will uncover any areas of concern, or will give a broad assurance that the contract is running smoothly, assists in their discharging of accountability requirements. If a public sector manager can point to an audit report, showing that he is making regular checks of performance/operations and acting on any results, he is taking proper steps to making his own management transparent and open.

Forensic/Contentious Audits

Forensic audits, or audits performed in a hostile contract environment, are the diametrical opposite of straightforward performance/compliance audit. Undertaking an audit in the face of contractor hostility is painful, time consuming, unnecessary and costly. Undertaking a forensic audit, with a client perception of potential fraud, can be a rough experience for all concerned. Contentious audits are a sub-set of a forensic audit, as it is undoubtedly true that no contractor will welcome any process specifically looking to uncover fraud.

The issue of fraud in itself is a separate subject. The making of profit, or its maximisation within a contract, is not fraudulent. Fraud is when misappropriation of funds in some way is entailed – that is, embezzlement, sub-contractor preferment, bribery, procedural or accounting manipulation in the contractor's interest. However, having said that, an examination of overhead and profit are usually the first points of enquiry for any examination of financial fraud.

Given that this book is about performance auditing, another take on forensic auditing is where an element of performance can be potentially fraudulent in itself. Here, a non-action is potentially fraudulent if the contractor is charging for a service it knowingly is not providing. Further, an action can be fraudulent if a contractor knowingly increases his profit level at the expense of the performance of a service.

However, to be clear, forensic/contentious audits are undertaken:

- in the certain knowledge of the contractor's true hostility and corporate intransigence to the process;

- where the audit is specifically meant to uncover areas of non-compliance (and this would include fraud) which might result in very punitive actions being taken.

The ramifications of audits constructed to unearth specific fault, or undertaken in the context of contractor hostility to the process, are discussed below. Forensic auditing demands a range of techniques and approaches to the subject under consideration. Conducting an audit in a contractually contentious situation means that information is likely to be difficult to recover, and the audit itself is likely to be time-consuming and fraught.

THE HOSTILE CONTRACTOR

We once started an audit with the threat of legal action. In this case, the contractor absolutely denied the public sector the right to look at his management records, and refused to turn them over for inspection. Arguments in this case were relatively simple, given the contractual reality that the building records belonged to the public sector. Our client at the time was strong and determined not to be dissuaded. The ultimatum of legal action was given with a clear deadline and the records duly arrived.

We have undertaken audits where it was apparently decided by contractor management that if no records were presented, then we wouldn't be able to comment (and so the audit would achieve a 'pass' grade). The level of non-compliance in this case was assessed in the mid 90 per cent, the plan backfired, and the audit was delivered before deadline, for far less cost.

We have started, and finished, audits over a period of some months, where the contractor would continually find reasons why something couldn't be presented when it was scheduled. As our client remained relatively content, so did we, and more so because of our certain knowledge that every move made by the contractor was clearly giving them even less room to manoeuvre (as it became increasingly difficult to provide information that did not directly contradict that given previously).

Most contractors we have met have been ill-prepared for the process. Even though all public sector contracts contain a 'right to audit' clause(s), contractors seem to be generally unaware of the necessity for the audit, what an audit might really entail, and what their client will expect of them during any audit process. As our brief case study on a government department's long-term audit strategy will show below, having an FM Contractor well aware that the Department has chosen to consistently audit over years, means that few surprises will be had when the process starts up with any new contract.

We might say an obvious thing here too – FM Contractors sometimes seem to feel that bringing an aggressive attitude to any audit party will intimidate auditors, or buy them room to manoeuvre in terms of data presentation. To be sure, entering into such an aggressive situation is not particularly for the faint-hearted. More likely than being intimidated, though, such a management strategy is likely to make the auditors particularly interested to know what, exactly, the contractor is trying to hide (and the contractor's client equally so). An aggressive response to a legitimate audit process is simply seen as unnecessarily obstructive and unprofessional. There is no gain in any contractor's doing so.

In practical terms, having a contractor directly hostile to the audit team simply eats up more time, but doesn't (generally) stop the process. If a contractor proves to be hostile, it is a given that the client side management team will become more involved in insisting on compliance with the audit team's requests. Part of a contractor's strategy in resisting an audit can be to throw up all sorts of spurious reasons why it shouldn't happen, and countering these arguments will always take up client time.

Any good auditor will advise his client at the outset of the possibility of needing his intervention at different times in the audit – upfront, during and subsequent. It is of fundamental importance that, if the contractual relationships are confrontationally based, that the client management team is clear about their potential strategy to cope with a contractor who could fight the audit all the way to its conclusion. A strong client here will continue to be relaxed but firm in his determination to protect the public purse by checking that all is well with service provision.

While delaying an audit is not fatal, withdrawing an audit intention is, as the contractor will be correct in thinking that the client management team is not sufficiently strong to enter into any kind of dispute (and therefore, he can continue to work to his own agenda in FM management).

THE FORENSIC AUDIT

INTOSAI (the International Association of Supreme Audit Institutions) defines forensic auditing as: 'the application of auditing skills to situations that have legal consequences.' INTOSAI then categorises the types of forensic audits as:

- Proactive (which can be applied to the specific audit 'types' below, but is meant to uncover malpractice before it has an overwhelming effect).

- Statutory (to look at compliance with laws and regulations).

- Regulatory (concerning the proper distribution of funds).

- Diagnostic (to highlight risks arising either out of fraud or from any other source).

- Investigatory (to respond to complaints or suspicions of malpractice).

- Reactive (to specifically examine specific areas of suspected fraud).

The point about proactive forensic auditing is worth reinforcing. Auditors will always look for malpractice as part of any audit subject, but will not specifically drill down into the subject without client agreement. This is to say that any VFM/ performance/compliance audit will naturally include looking at the subject under consideration for any serious malpractice, as part of their primary task. A public sector property manager should understand this, and communicate (if he wishes) that this is automatically incorporated within any wider-context audit commissioned. This proactive approach costs little in terms of time, but will provide the earliest possible warning if systems/actions are dubious, or open to misuse.

As with almost every situation in auditing, the point here is that of nuance. A VFM/performance audit is simply an audit meant to establish if performance and contract spend is satisfactory. However, any VFM/performance audit naturally does concern itself with compliance with all industry and public sector practices and policies, and so any digression from those norms will invite an audit comment. If an auditor sees something truly disturbing, any client can rest assured that he will be informed as to its ramifications very early (before any formal report). The differentiation here is a performance audit will naturally, but relatively casually, look for evidence of malpractice as an adjunct to the overall audit task, but a forensic audit will take the uncovering of misconduct as its primary theme.

To our mind, simply, forensic auditing is where one tries to look beneath the area under inspection, to see its functioning or construct in the truest sense. INTOSAI published their observations on forensic auditing in 1996, and recognised that many problems exist in the undertaking of such audits – the need for clear protocols, a true separation of auditor/audit subject, and the use of Information Technology to uncover patterns of behaviour. INTOSAI recommended, at the conclusion of their paper, that the provision of a forensic auditing methodology would be of use in public sector auditing to provide more guidance for those looking to uncover malpractice.

Given that any audit is structured with terms and briefs conditional to the contractual situation, so are forensic audits. While INTOSAI are correct in recommending a framework methodology, any methodology would need to be altered to correctly reflect any individual subject matter or contract. Therefore, practically, any public sector manager looking to commission a forensic audit, of whatever type, should look for auditors who are technically excellent and have the resources to deal with one of the most demanding auditing tasks that exist. In a sense, having found and commissioned any team, the audit process will continue like any other. The audit team will formally investigate the area concerned and report back on schedule with the required detailed analysis.

If we consider that forensic auditing is looking for any clear evidence that might exist of malpractice having financial consequences for the contract owner, then another guiding principle must be if the public sector is paying a sum for the provision of contractually defined services, the public sector has every right to know that it is receiving the exact service purchased. This receipt of service includes understanding fully if delegated responsibilities are being adhered to and discharged according to all relevant law and contractually defined business and public sector policy requirements.

Forensic auditing of public sector property contracts can ask questions to uncover deliberate management actions that might used systematically to benefit a contractor. The examples here are many, but can include areas where profitability increases unfairly through hidden overcharging, or an economy of scale not being declared and so on:

- inappropriate management percentages added on to manage works;

- management fees being added twice or more for works/tasks undertaken by sister companies;

- charging for a service/part of a service that is deliberately withheld;

- the use of substandard materials, while charging for those of a greater quality;

- the packaging of works so that a greater management fee can be charged;

- the sharing of resources/personnel across contracts, but full rates being charged for this part-time provision.

Forensic auditing also takes the view, from the outset, of deep suspicion, and any audit team will be primarily concerned about any ways the contract can be abused individually or corporately.

A situation once arose in an audit where there were concerns that corporate friends of the FM contractor were being used as sub-contractors without client agreement, with unpublished rates, and without any internal vetting procedures. We were asked to examine sub-contractor lists to see if those concerns were valid. Without giving much away, we found that the concern was probably true – some companies were traced to residential addresses, for example. Here, the client had a discreet word with his contractor and expressed his unhappiness. The sub-contractor list did change fairly rapidly.

Forensic auditing is normally concerned with financial transactions, but contains techniques which can also be used to confirm VFM or adherence to performance standards. While all audits are always constructed on hard data (that is, data that can be clearly examined by another to reach the same conclusion), a forensic audit uses this data with the full recognition that this data may be used in the construction of a case that could go to law. In that sense, the audit team enters into the audit project with all applicable regulations and legislation firmly in their mind, and will place all evidence found clearly within that context.

Another audit was undertaken some time ago to examine if unequivocal statements made by an FM contractor about the accuracy of Helpdesk data was accurate. Using a variety of techniques, including line-by-line reading of Helpdesk records, and looking in detail as to how the system could be subverted, we found that the entire system was open to misuse, and unequivocal statements about performance actuality could never be made while it remained so. In this case, a prolonged argument between the contractor/client broke out and a great time of misery for all concerned ensued. Ultimately, financial redress was achieved because of the accuracy of our findings.

A forensic audit looking at performance/VFM will look to see if the service is being delivered at the original tendered price and will seek to understand that the service is purposeful within the contract. This is to say that an element of non-compliance in this context should be a service that is too lightly delivered to be meaningful (CCTV being used, for example, but with no monitoring taking place). In this case then, the public sector would be paying for a service not being received, and the Contract Sum should be adjusted accordingly, or the service re-instituted (and recompense given for the period of time it was not provided).

In practice, undertaking a forensic audit is to continuously look laterally at the area under examination, and this includes financial forensic audits. One is reminded of Dr. John Grierson's observation on art: 'If you can roll it downhill and nothing falls off, its art'. In this case, if you can roll an audit element downhill and nothing falls off, all is well.

Now, by 'rolling downhill', of course we mean:

- that the subject is examined from every conceivable angle to determine its robustness/openness to misuse: financially, legislatively, managerially, administratively, practically;

- that the subject is considered specifically for any possible way it can be subverted (where a system is open to ready misuse by any body because of the fragility of the system itself);

- that all records perfectly mesh and are meaningful, but show no sign of being created specifically for the audit;

- that hypothetical situations are posited and tested against the system, to determine whether or not a system can accommodate practices or actions it should not (a non-trained engineer, for example, or the use of a friend to deliver goods without any market-testing/corporate vetting).

To look at a specific example, in a forensic audit looking at PPM we would want to look at some or all of the following, in addition to the points above:

- What the relationships are between PPM/reactive maintenance and small works, as the concepts are interrelated and can financially have a significant impact on client spend (for example, lax maintenance can trigger plant replacement/works which could financially benefit the contractor).

- Through a broader sampling, track individual engineers to assess what work is accomplished in sample days against the need of the PPM job sheet in itself (to ascertain if engineer's time is being double-booked, and therefore staff costs being charged twice, or if engineering staffing overall could be reduced, or if maintenance cannot be seen to be taking place but still charged).

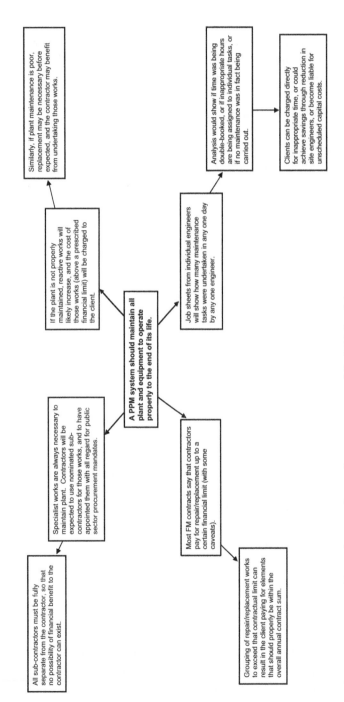

Figure 3.2 Outline of some forensic tests on specific PPM subjects

- Look in some detail at any 'comprehensive' element of the contract (where the contractor pays for any element of plant and equipment up to a certain financial level) to ascertain if that contractual mandate is being adhered to, or if packaging of work occurs so that the client pays for something it should not.

- Look at 'call off' contracts used for engineering or any other specialist tasks. Have the firms been properly vetted, carry the relevant industry quality accreditations, and have a competitive schedule of rates published and regularly updated? Do the firms exist? (This, to confirm that all sub-contractors are valid separate identities from the FM Contractor, and so that the FM company does not benefit inappropriately directly from their use.)

Graphically, the examples can be shown opposite:

In respect of cleaning contracts, as another example, we would want to look at some or all of the following, dependent on any specific client concerns:

- How are cleaners hired? How does the contractor know that staff allowed on site (typically overnight) are appropriately security cleared/vetted? How does the contractor arrange for a pool of vetted staff to be available to cover absences? How does the contractor know that only those who are appropriately vetted are those truly in attendance (we would want to know if only appropriate people are allowed on site, and that steps are in place to prohibit entry passes being passed around)?

- How management checks are made – what level of supervision exists on site, and is this supported by unambiguous record keeping (clients will be charged for this management function, and it would seem automatically difficult for a pool of cleaners to work well without supervision)?

To illustrate:

Forensic audits, in the broadest possible sense, can be seen as compliance audits writ large. Looking at an audit approach here, auditors commence a forensic audit knowing that they will need to state very clearly opinions that might have the most serious ramifications. All care is always taken in every audit. In a

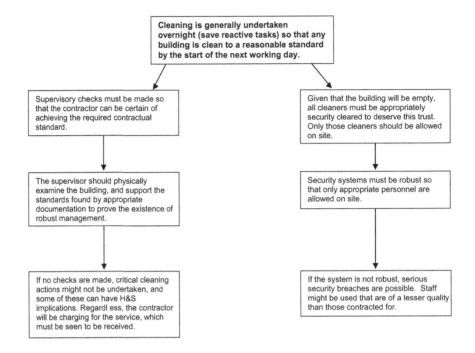

Figure 3.3   **Outline of some forensic tests on a cleaning service**

forensic audit, this care can extend into carefully placing any negative findings into the hands of lawyers, and for all other appropriate action to be taken by third parties.

Partnering Audits

Partnering audits are audits that are constructed knowing that client/contractor relations are strong, and where the two generally work together as a coordinated team. It is possible, and can be beneficial, for an audit to be undertaken in a partnering sense with the contractor – with all caveats of audit independence remaining intact.

By an audit taking place in 'a partnering sense' we mean a circumstance where:

- the client/contractor management team have an open and frank relationship which is positive and constructive;

- the contract itself can be seen, through other means, to be broadly on course and largely compliant with its requirements;

- the contract is not old and not new, and so that there is still much to be gained by all from any 'lessons learned' that result from the audit.

Within these broad categorisations then, the audit brief would be to be as open as possible with the contractor about the audit intentions, so that the contractor can readily see the context of the forthcoming exercise. The audit brief would be shared relatively openly, so that the contractor can see the underlying purpose of the audit, and so they can see the value the exercise might have for the public sector and ultimately even, for themselves. This sharing – to lapse back into cynicism – would be done at a point sufficiently close for the scheduled audit so that only the most basic contractor management actions could be done to prepare.

The value of a partnering approach – and Communities and Local Government (CLG) have been very successful here – is that the contractor is most likely to buy-in to audit results if it can see the foundation for the exercise. The partnering approach, however, starts and stops at particular points. The audit team will work independently during the audit itself, before resuming its open discussion at its conclusion.

Depending on the state-of-play of the contract, a client can reasonably request their audit team to effectively preview the entire course of the audit in advance. This is most reasonably done when the client wishes the contractor not to be able to claim any lack of comprehension as to why the audit is looking at a particular subject in question.

An example here might be where the client wishes the contractor to be clear why minor works procurement must be transparent and within all local and national mandates. In this example, it is valid for the client to use its auditor as a best practice guide and so, when the audit comes, the contractor can (effectively) follow the process in real time and without managerial obfuscation.

In one instance, we were requested to spend a day with a contractor for an unrecorded 'mini audit', and with the client in attendance. During the mini-audit, we were requested to walk the contractor through how we approached our understanding of the subject concerned. The contractor was invited to follow our thinking and processes, and ask questions. The client strategy was that the contractor could make clear improvements in advance of the next audit on the subject, with maximum clarity as to what was expected for the provision of the service/management information. The strategy was wholly constructive, in that it did inform and shape future improvements without jeopardising any confidentiality.

Using an auditor as a resource for productive advice is a good example of a partnering approach. As all audit commentary is always based on generally available information (industry standards, best practice and legislative requirements), making the process of how compliance is assessed is helpful to all, and does not divulge anything that isn't common knowledge.

A partnering audit can be also conducted fairly openly on site, dependent on the subject and on one's client's wishes. While no auditor we have met will discuss conclusions in advance of any report being presented to client, it is possible to draw contractor attention to individual items as they are being seen – again, so that contractor buy-in effectively starts at time of audit. Minor works procurement is a good example: there is no way that any contractor can falsify historic procurement records, so conversations about individual issues can be held without compromising the ability for future audits of historic records.

Specifically, as an example again, if we found that a sub-contractor was being used repeatedly, but without being on any pre-approval list of suitable specialists, there is no harm in asking why that might be so (and therefore, the contractor being able to see that a comment is likely to be made on the subject in due course). In this case, auditors will know that there will be no physical way that records of historic procurement can be altered – invoices for the service/goods will have been long received.

Similarly, the client can choose to have the contractor present at any informal debrief scheduled. While a pre-report debrief is simply a matter for the client to decide upon – if they wish an advance notice of likely outcomes – it is not at all mandatory, and might be discouraged by the auditor dependent on the audit's findings. If, however, the public sector manager feels that the exercise is sufficiently important, an informal debrief allows for any correction of fact, and for all to begin taking steps to progress in advance of the formal report. Here, the contractor can demonstrably see that the partnering element of the contract remains strong, as he and the client team are present together to consider draft findings simultaneously. In terms of an overall management strategy, therefore, an informal debrief can assist in cementing an existing good relationship, and has the further benefit of saving time and more detailed management involvement.

Modular Audits

Modular audits are audits that are constructed using set parameters, so that data can be directly compared over time. Modular audits can be used to regularly examine one building, or an estate. The use of modular audits can be valuable to an organisation looking to regularly audit their properties over a determined period, and are not a valid construct for any one-off audit situation.

Modular audits have positive attributes:

- They allow for direct comparison of answers to identical audit questions, so that improvements/deterioration in performance can be clearly seen.

- Their modular nature does allow for issues to enter and exit the audit process, so that concentration on any one area under consideration can be readily accomplished.

- They provide for greater surety for both client and contractor as to expectations of any audit or series of audits.

- They reduce the auditor learning curve, or time spent in audit construction – so leading to economies in commissioning any audit.

Modular audits have parallel negatives:

- They are not appropriate for a one-off/short-lived audit programme, as the time spent setting up a valid modular system will be disproportionate to the audit(s) itself.

- The modular nature of the audit means that the audit itself is less able to approach any subject laterally, and so to look deeper at any process/problem found to be questionable.

- The relative certainty to the audit process that the modular construct brings, might allow a contractor to over-prepare in known areas, and therefore hide true compliance levels (knowing that other questions are unlikely to be asked).

The decision to commission a modular audit structure, however, can be overwhelmingly positive for a client management team. While more time will be spent in the audit construction than is usual, the end result will be an audit structure that can be undertaken by any professional and that will produce results that will remain valid in almost any circumstance.

Modular audit structures are meant to provide building blocks of key audit questions that can be brought in and out, or remain intact over time. If a downside to a modular audit is its inherent lack of auditor discretion in an audit, an upside is that it does provide sufficient flexibility to examine a breadth of subjects over time.

For example:

If an FM contract has recently been let, commissioning a modular audit structure will provide a road map for understanding overall contractual compliance over the course of its tenure. The relatively clear-cut statements of compliance will show directly comparable trend analysis of compliance/non-compliance in specific areas of service provision.

To illustrate here, the types of questions that would be put in a modular audit would be:

- Are lease issues reviewed regularly and necessary actions scheduled? The answer would simply be yes/no, and with no detailed examination if the necessary actions were well-considered (rather than simply scheduled). Any break in reviewing lease necessities (such as structural maintenance) would show a shortfall in performance.

- Are H&S risk assessments up-to-date and have they been disseminated to staff? The answers would be yes/no, based on:

  - any changes to H&S legislation being reflected in the risk assessments;

- timely adherence to the FM contractors own Quality Management procedures for revisiting of H&S records;
- dated copies of risk assessments in service stream manager's possession.

• What are the numbers of customer complaints on a service-by-service basis? Here, a simple count would be performed, showing any increases or decreases, but no probing would take place as to any circumstances for the complaint being registered. The answers, however, would allow for trend analysis of complaints overall.

To illustrate further, the diagram below shows the relative strengths and weaknesses of a modular versus bespoke performance audit structures, on a sample audit of forward works planning.

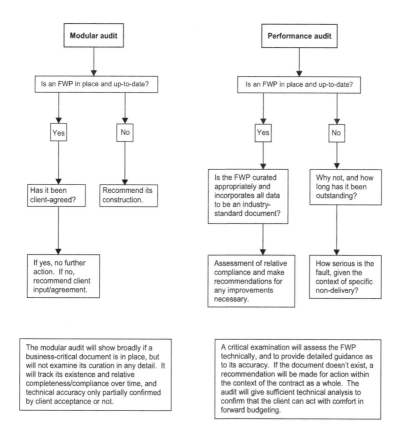

Figure 3.4   **Outline of the strengths and weaknesses of modular versus bespoke performance audit**

The diagram above shows that a client will receive more detailed analysis in a bespoke FM performance audit. While there is no reason why a modular audit cannot also pose more detailed questions, doing so reduces the reasons why a modular format would be chosen in the first place.

If a modular audit looked to probe deeper into any areas of non-compliance, the kinds and amounts of prose needed to support any conclusions drawn, will reduce the clear-cut 'yes/no' audit answers. At that point, the modular construct starts to deteriorate. The audit explanations will provide sufficient caveats for to the 'yes/no' assessment that results will become difficult to compare.

The overwhelming benefit of a modular audit construct, however, is significant in the circumstances appropriate to it. The 'yes/no' unequivocal audit statements allow for a clear assessment of overall compliance over time – and this is of value in itself. While a 'yes' to an FWP being in place is no guarantee of the FWP being of any industry-standard quality, the FWP will have been seen in the audit and it will have been seen as resembling an FWP. This is to say that, even with the cursory view taken in this type of audit, an auditor will ensure that the document held is a Forward Works Plan, and does represent the building/estate concerned (while not probing any further).

The modular structure can also have a series of contributory questions that would allow for greater concentration on any area as required.

For example, in the diagram above, subsidiary questions could also be drafted for the modular audit strand, all of which would be confirmed as true or not:

- Is the condition survey of the building still extant and reflected in the FWP?

- Is the asset register updated on a daily/weekly/monthly basis?

- Are client policy requirements being reflected as required?

- Are regular assessments being made of works staying in, or moving out of the FWP?

These simple additional questions will give a clearer view on whether or not the FWP is a live document, rather than an irrelevant piece of data. They will still allow for comparison over time, as the yes/no responses will indicate a more detailed level of compliance without compromising the point of the modular structure (to avoid explanatory prose, and simply track the general adequacy, point-blank, over time).

Summary

Audits can deliver broad or very detailed assurance on any issue relating to building management.

Wide-ranging performance audits will use sampling techniques to provide an overview on any contract's overall compliance with contractual provisions, and will provide commentary on any individual issues found. The client can then decide if and when these issues should be followed up by a further examination. A performance audit will provide detailed technical assurance on the subject matter, and so provide the client with data needed to further manage the contract.

Forensic audits are generally constructed to unearth, definitively, inappropriate activity in the management of a building. Different techniques are used here, so that any potential/actual misuse of public funds can be ascertained. These audits tend to be conducted in a hostile environment, which are likely to have further knock-on effects to the overall management regime.

Partnering audits can be wholly constructive in the right circumstances. Partnering audits assume a greater degree of contractor buy-in, and have positive management attributes. These audits assume working relatively openly with the contractor, and so that faster improvements can be made.

Modular audits are a worthwhile investment for any FM contract with some time to run. These audits can provide directly comparable broadly-based assurance that the FM house is in order, while not providing any detailed analysis of the quality of the work itself. Modular audits can limit management input into the process, and provide a reasonable amount of assurance to the management team that public funds are being spent appropriately as all business critical documents are in place.

4

The Audit Environment: Setting the Context

'An auditor is a man who watches the battle from the safety of the hills and then comes down to bayonet the wounded.'
Sir Charles Lyell 1797 — 1875, British lawyer and geologist.

Introduction

While most audits will tend to be a mixture of styles — where an element of an audit might be examined forensically, and other elements discussed more freely with the audit subject — deciding an overall audit construct is a fundament of any audit commission. This chapter provides guidelines for how the public sector might choose to commission an audit, and the overall ramifications of any chosen approach.

Any auditor will want to understand some basic information before providing an opinion on the best way forward. This basic information will range from specific contractual information, to their client's sense of their business relationship with the contractor concerned. Any good auditor looking to plan an audit will want to understand as fully as possible all expectations, and so that neutral advice can be best given as to the best audit strategy, construct and eventual fulfilment.

The earlier chapters have looked at how audits are conducted overall in terms of overarching audit approaches and constructs. This chapter will look at the subject in more detail. For simplicity's sake, we will use the overall types of audit outlined above — performance, forensic, partnering and modular — as continuous references here. However, and this must be obvious, the reality is that all property audits contain elements of all 'types' the majority of the time.

Pre-Audit — Choosing the Audit Form

OVERALL FACTORS TO CONSIDER

Audits tend to be conducted in the teeth of shifting policy, shifting personnel, shifting priorities and VFM concerns — normal everyday public sector business. Within any ever-changing public sector business, however, the need to understand the effectiveness of a contract's performance remains. The choice of audit subjects, contexts and approaches are many and varied, and management decisions will always need to be made as to the place of audit within the overall workings of public sector estate management.

Another constant is that most contractors are likely to be less-than-pleased about the audit due to take place, for all legitimate and semi-legitimate reasons (and these reasons are scattered throughout this book). Client-side understanding of their contractor's management style is important to assist in determining upfront how contractor management is likely to interact with any one-off audit or audit programme. Client understanding of their contractor management norms will inform how they might need to react and manage the event themselves.

Many FM property contracts are explicitly developed and let to be 'Partnering Contracts'. A common public sector/contractor misunderstanding of this positive management stance is that an audit cannot/should not be necessary when any partnering element of the contract is strong. The temptation on the client side is to not rock the boat, and trust in the positive statements made by its partner. In general, however, the temptation of unqualified reliance on contractor data should be resisted. Appropriate checks of performance are reasonable. Audits can be positive, and in any case, are a pre-requisite of the public sector satisfying itself that all is well and to the degree that their contractor says they are.

Of course, some audits are notified to the contractor in the guise of the audit being a necessary evil, and the audit team as the agents of this unfortunate requirement. This is to say that, in the example where it is expedient to achieve the corporate aim of confirming compliance/performance/VFM and so on whilst keeping good client/contractor relations, most auditors will feel it acceptable to be cast as something foisted upon the client, rather than as a deliberate choice by the management team (if it assists the end result).

The version of good cop/bad cop is an old ploy that continues to work. Auditors are perfectly accustomed to being 'bad cop' in any circumstance that is legitimate to achieve the desired aim. Bad cop means that the truly hard things about performance that need to be said, can be said clearly, while the client is allowed to express their sympathy and work constructively with the contractor to improve performance. This is an overwhelmingly positive aspect to the ploy, and can be very effective in maintaining a steady ship, while the auditors/bad cops drive through change.

There is an added advantage here, where this completely legitimate strategy is not far from the truth. Auditors will never have any vested interest in any audit. Clients, of course, may have to work with the same contractor management team over years to come, and where the ability to retain good overall management relationships is important. Part of a public sector management consideration can legitimately be to determine whether its ostensible separation from the audit process can be of use over the short-medium term, in their ongoing contract management.

When an audit does go ahead — or even better, a scheduled series of audits progresses — client side will begin to have a range of performance data available that has different, far reaching uses.

How to Decide the Best Audit Approach

Deciding an audit approach is an audit tactic that any performance auditor will consider and advise upon, before any confirmation of brief is fed back to his/her client. While an audit approach directly informs all aspects of the auditing task itself, this approach also directly reflects what the client wishes to discover, the state of the client's relationship with his contractor, and the nature of the contract itself.

An audit approach means the overall audit structure, and with subsidiary management and performance contributory factors to it. An audit can be horizontal or vertical, micro or macro, VFM-based, a sample health-check, a rigorous compliance or forensic audit, and other examples. An audit can be undertaken relatively openly, or firmly behind doors closed to all.

An audit approach also infers a state of mind on the auditor, in that knowingly entering a contractual situation where all parties are on the cusp of litigation, for example, will affect how any audit is approached in the first place. While none of the core principles of audit are affected by the choice of one approach over another, the audit approach does define a superstructure and wider terms of reference for the specific audit to be carried out.

Typically, an audit is prepared and outlines constructed through discussions with the client-side management team. An auditor is called in for a general discussion about the proposed project, the auditor feeds back what he can at the time, then goes away to propose an audit brief — so far, so obvious. Much information will influence any auditor's recommendations for an audit structure, or audit approach. Any of the answers below will influence what an auditor will feel might usefully be discovered, how, and to what end.

For example, an audit at the end of a contract's life can be useful in terms of 'lessons learned' for the future, but will not radically affect any part of its running on site. Similarly, a general health check of performance overall may not discover individual faults in a detailed technical management protocol. A contract that is ostensibly running smoothly may not be so in truth, and so a more vertical audit on a service stream might assist in understanding any hidden underlying issues.

Each approach demands different methodologies from the audit team. Each approach will provide different levels of detail on the subject matter. Each approach demands a different time commitment by the auditors, and by client management.

In order to advise on an audit construct, the auditor will want to know, in terms of overview/as a starting point, the answers to the following questions:

- Where are we in terms of the contract's tenure — the beginning, middle or end? What is the size of the estate it covers, numbers of personnel? Is the contract a Total FM Contract, or are some functions retained by the public sector?

- What is the context for the client deciding to commission a performance audit now? Is the decision because of general concerns, specific suspicions/problems encountered or a change in client-side management (for example)?

- What scope of audit does the client have in mind? Is the audit to cover hard and soft services, Health & Safety compliance, management records, confirmation of VFM, or a combination, or all?

- What is the overall history of the contract's functioning? Has a regular programme of client-side monitoring taken place to date and, if so, what results have been seen? Is the contract self-monitoring and, if so, has the client checked their contractor's own assessment of their performance?

- Are there specific technical problems or areas of concern? Does the client need specific confirmation of compliance/performance in particular areas?

- How are client/contractor relations in general? Does the client have confidence in the FM management team? Is the contract working well in a partnering sense, or are relationships difficult and confrontational?

- How are hard services running? What is the age of the building(s) under the contract? Does the client have confidence in the planned/reactive maintenance taking place?

- What are the business- or mission-critical factors?

- How does client-feedback take place? Does the client know, through any formal means, if end-users are content with the service?

- Any timing or budgetary constraints? Is there a need for a fast cursory view, or a more in-depth exploration? When would the client like to see the draft report?

The client will want to know at the time of first meeting:

- any initial thoughts the auditor might have in terms of recommending approaches to the subject confirmed;

- any experience the auditor has which might assist in determining the audit brief;

- timing (of the audit and to report), the potential audit team members and rough cost.

In broad terms, however, we could look at the conduct of an audit in four general ways — in terms of its overall approach. Set out below are four scenarios, based on a broad outline of a straightforward performance audit, a forensic audit, a partnering audit, and a modular audit. The four scenarios are meant to illustrate further how different influences and instructions do affect how an auditor is likely to approach the task at hand.

How Instructions Might Differ and Their Impact

To understand how an audit instruction can directly impact on the ongoing conduct of the contract, it might be useful to undertake a rudimentary risk assessment, as below.

The chart gives a basic idea of what one might expect in terms of the impacts of any audit on management time and change in the contract itself. Any public sector body looking to commission an audit should do so fully aware of the impact the audit might have on peripheral issues, as well as the audit's possibility of impacting on the contract's operation over time.

Client brief	Contractor buy-in	Potential effect on contract over time	Potential for rapid redress	Impact on client management time	Impact on client management post-audit
Confirm compliance/ performance with major contractual terms	Medium — this is a natural occurrence in any contract	High — regular compliance/ performance audits can instigate improvements in systems and on the ground	High (for any H&S/statutory maintenance issues) — Low (for any small issues with service delivery)	Low — the audit should be non-controversial, and input will be needed (on the whole) at the beginning and end of the audit	Medium — any change management plan produced will require oversight and/or appropriate follow-up
Forensic audit to understand any serious malpractice	Low — even if there is nothing to hide	High — even if no malpractice is found, relations between client/ contractor will change	High — dependent on outcomes and client will	High — it is likely that the auditors will require ongoing contact or that the contractor will attempt to stop the process	High — including the potential for legal action/senior management resolution time
Partnering audit to work constructively to problem solve any issues found	High — the contractor is treated as an (almost) equal partner	Medium — change is not forced, but negotiated point by point	Medium — change is not forced, but negotiated point by point	Medium — the client and contractor will work together in its construct and execution	Medium — any change management plan produced will require oversight and/or appropriate follow-up
Modular audit to regularly discover base contractual compliance.	High — the contractor will have reasonable knowledge of the ongoing process	Medium — relatively crude compliance levels will be routinely assessed, but deeper non-compliance may remain invisible	High — the point blank assessment allows for no ambiguity	Low — having agreed the audit construct the client will only need to monitor results over time	Medium — if a failure is found, the non-compliance is likely to be fairly severe and demand time to resolve

How Can You Tell What Type of Audit Might Best Suit Your Contract and the Information You Wish to Uncover?

The examples below outline a few broad hypotheses on natural contractual situations, and with comment as to how an auditor might describe how the audit process would impact on the issue. The examples give a general guide to a clear choice of audit construct in specific circumstances.

Contractual situation	Audit process
The contract has never been audited/not been audited for some time	A performance audit, covering a wide range of subjects on a sampling basis will give an overall comment on adherence to base contractual issues
Specific assurances need to be given to an Accounting Officer that all is in order on the contract	A performance audit containing that requirement will probe quite widely and deeply, including performance and financial matters, so that specific assurances can be given with confidence
The contract was audited some time ago, some difficult issues were uncovered, and confirmation is needed that change has occurred and/or to force that change	A follow-up performance audit can readily cover old ground and use the time passed to make a stronger comment if necessary on lack of progress
The contract has just been let, and we have sufficient faith in contractor management systems that all will be well. We would like, however, to establish a programme that provides overarching assurance that all documentation/systems are in place	A modular audit structure can be established that will regularly monitor if record keeping and input into the management process is on schedule and as contracted
The contract Manager has some low-level undefined concerns that some activities are not taking place	A performance audit will discover if those concerns are justified, in a broad sense, or not
Charges are being put through that do not appear to have a contractual basis for presentation, but are presented as a fait accompli (with works complete)	A forensic audit will uncover any issues with overpayment/inappropriate payment
Variations have not been formalised over time, and we are unsure if the variations are now appropriate within the contract as a whole (or if the requested variation should now be eliminated)	A forensic audit will discover if any variations are appropriate within the contract, have been properly agreed and priced, and the ramifications on the clients long-term financial responsibilities
No evidence has been seen regarding self-certification despite repeated requests	A forensic audit will discover if all managerial checks are being made by the contractor according to contract, and will recommend redress if they are not (that is, if the services cannot be seen to be delivered as required)
We believe we are being overcharged for small works	A forensic audit will discover if procurement is legitimate, and that all on-costs are market-reasonable and according to contract
The relationship between client and contractor is strong, and confirmation is sought to confirm openly that all is running as it should	A partnering audit can be structured so that its conduct is relatively open, and so that the contractor can see clearly through its progression results that are likely to be found
We like the idea of a relatively open audit, but do not wish any results to be shared/clear as they are found	A partnering audit can be conducted as such, but to also keep elements as private between the audit team/client

Understanding the Context

Naturally, an auditor will want to know the basic contract-specific issues on which any audit will fit within — the context of the contract overall.

Understanding the contract's context means, to an auditor:

- How long the contract has been operational, and when is it due for re-let?

- What is the scope of the contract, in terms of services and the size of the estate?

- What is the contract Sum, and if it has been varied?

- Is the contract based on self-assessment that is checked/not checked by the client, or is there a formal internal/external audit programme, or none of the above?

- Is there a management partnering approach, and is this working well or not? If not, why not?

- What does the client hope to achieve from the audit(s)?

The purpose of an initial discussion with a prospective auditor is to provide a broad overview of the contract, and to feed the auditor as much information as possible about its overall state-of-play. This base information will help the auditors to advise best on audit approaches that might be most useful to their public sector client.

To illustrate how different answers to the above questions might impact on what audit approach might be taken, the following hypothetical scenarios might be of some use. The examples show a range of possibilities, and with an auditor's likely reaction to it, in terms of advice.

CONTRACT TENURE

- The contract is one year old, and has another 4 years to run for its initial term.

The contract is new, and while systems should have 'bedded in', there is likely to be varied and variable data available. A health check might be of use, to discover if the transition from the old regime to the new worked well, and if basic systems operations are robust.

- The contract is 5 years old, with a further 20 to run.

This PFI Contract should be well established, lines of reportage should be clear, and the contract should be running smoothly. A compliance/performance check would be worthwhile to ensure that end-users are content, management procedures are robust, and that no unforeseen liabilities exist.

- The contract is 6 years old, and a new procurement exercise is underway for the new contract edition.

At this late point in the contract it may be worthwhile to keep a closer, albeit light touch, eye on the in-situ contractor, as staff morale will continue to decrease in the run-up to the new contract let. Spot checks of critical services would be useful for the client team, in order to advise the contract procurement team that data affecting the new let is robust.

CONTRACT SCOPE

- The contract encompasses all FM Services on an estate of 3 buildings.

A performance audit can give fairly detailed assurances on the contract overall in a relatively short period of time (as the estate is small).

- The contract encompasses all FM Services on an estate of 25 buildings across the South East.

Undertaking a comprehensive performance audit across 25 buildings is a complex, time-consuming and costly exercise. Sampling of management systems and reportage up to client and chasing data back to its origin on site (that is, for site verification of accuracy) will provide a reasonable indication — based on identified percentile samplings — if there are any broader reasons for concern or not.

- The contract encompasses only hard services on an estate of 10 buildings.

The estate is quite large, but hard services are a discrete specialist area. An auditor is likely to propose to pick two or three discrete sub-sections of hard services provision where compliance is vital (statutory inspections, or safety rules and procedures, for example) and examine them in detail. If all is robust, the client should feel moderately content that the rest of the hard services provided for are likely to be similarly so. If problems are found, however, the auditor will recommend further investigations.

CONTRACT SUM

- The Contract Sum has not altered from contract let save for prescribed uplifts, and minor variations.

There is nothing to audit here in terms of verifying the accuracy of the Contract Sum. Views could be taken on other financial issues — reactive and comprehensive maintenance spend — for example, if this was of any concern. If the overall Contract Sum has not changed from contract let, it is axiomatic that the current Contract Sum corresponds with the original procurement exercise.

- The Contract Sum has varied significantly from contract let for a number of reasons.

A healthcheck of the Contract Sum would likely be appropriate, to ensure that variations were properly costed and agreed by the client management team.

EXISTING AUDIT PROGRAMME

- The contract is self-monitoring by the contractor and results are reported to the client team monthly — these results have not been formally checked.

An auditor would recommend a formal check of the data presented to the client, to confirm its accuracy. The auditor would recommend that regular checks are made of this data on a sampling basis by the client team or external auditor, the frequency of which would depend on the accuracy of the original exercise.

- The contract performance has been deemed to be satisfactory through Customer Satisfaction Surveys, and we have felt no need to probe any further.

Customer Satisfaction Surveys only paint a very limited picture of performance, and an auditor would recommend that further checks be made to assure the client management team that all is well with services not readily seen by building users — engineering maintenance, Health & Safety protocols, statutory inspections, management reportage, as examples.

- The contract was subject to a major audit on its 1st year anniversary (it is now Year 4 of the contract) and no formal audit has taken place since then.

A useful starting point here might be to see what progress was made on any recommendations contained in the Year 1 audit and from that, to see if other issues have arisen that require improvement. We would recommend that a fairly comprehensive annual audit of service delivery is a minimum requirement for FM Contracts.

- The contract has never been audited.

We would recommend that a considered audit programme should be started to deliver step-change confirmation of compliance and to provide any recommendations for change. Given that the contract has never been audited, an auditor would recommend that a percentage based overview is taken, and to then look at any further discrete areas found to be problematic on a scheduled basis.

CLIENT/CONTRACTOR RELATIONS

- The contract is based on a strong partnering relationship between the parties, where both seek to assist in problem-solving and no blame-culture exists.

The auditor will take this to mean that any audit will be non-controversial, and that he can expect full and open cooperation from the contractor throughout the process.

- The contract is based on the client management opinion that the FM Contractor should provide what he is contracted to provide. Contractor/client relations are formal and the contract is implemented to the letter.

The auditor will understand this to mean that the FM Contractor will be fully aware of his contractual responsibilities, and will probably interpret the audit as a hostile move by his client. The auditor will therefore be aware that information for audit will likely have to be insisted upon through reliance on the contract and (as a worst case) clause-by-clause insistence on cooperation.

- Relations between the client-side team and the FM Contractor are strained, due to a series of on-site circumstances over some time. Litigation has been contemplated, and the contractor is aware that an audit will take place to confirm the rights/wrongs of the issues leading to the potential dispute.

The auditor will take this circumstance as a formal forensic audit where all findings could result as contributory evidence in any formal dispute. The audit team would undertake the audit with a 'closed door' approach where any communication is made in writing, and other communications are limited. All data gathered would be carefully assessed against the contractual requirements, and applicable legislation/statutory requirements.

WHAT DOES THE CLIENT HOPE TO ACHIEVE THROUGH THE AUDIT?

- An immediate confirmation that all is well or not, in general terms, with the contract's performance.

The auditor would likely recommend a spot check across all key service provisions in the contract. This spot check, in its construct, would vary given the different technical natures and requirements of each service. The net result would be a limited guarantee of full compliance, but a considered view on whether the performance is likely to be 'reasonable' overall, or not.

- The start of a mid-term programme of regular audits, meant throughout their course to formally confirm that all is in order throughout the contract.

The auditor would develop a programme of audits for client approval, and would probably include a recommendation for a formal change-management programme. The auditor would take care that the audit programme was sufficiently varied so that the contractor could not readily predict what the next audit might consist of. Any change as a result of a previous audit would be briefly looked at in the subsequent exercise, to confirm that the change was robust and appropriate and satisfied the previous audit recommendations.

- A short sharp audit on a specific subject meant to compel improvement and compliance with the contract terms based on a client suspicion that all is not well.

The audit would examine the subject in the round, to be certain that the client's perspective on compliance was demonstrably correct, and then to forensically examine any deviations from the contract (and best practice/normal industry practice). Great care would be taken to understand the contractor's point of view on the subject, so that any formal comments could be countered or agreed with in the eventual report. The auditor would likely treat the assignment as potentially 'pre-dispute'.

Summary

In summary, an audit instruction and its subsidiary — an audit context — are frameworks for a formal exercise meant to discover a series of factual truths. A client wishing to understand how to instruct an auditor can, simply, be clear about what he wishes to discover, a timescale he must work to, and discuss the potential audit's context with his appointed auditor. Any auditor can take that information and provide a good brief that is fed back to his client, so any fine-tuning can be done on the instruction, or so that it forms the confidential basis on which the audit is to be undertaken.

The point of the above examples, and the preceding rudimentary risk assessment, is that one can approach commissioning an audit like an auditor would approach the audit itself — through a considered lateral view of the problems one wishes to understand. This is to say that any client wishing to commission an audit should understand that audit's affect on the contract's progression as a whole — including their own management time, the impact on relations with their contractor, and the likelihood of discovering, generally, what they wish through the technique and strategy identified.

A broadly based performance audit will not provide any assurance that no fraud is taking place. A forensic audit will not necessarily talk about site performance. A partnering audit will not automatically provide an insistence on rapid change, that rapid change being the subject of separate negotiations between the contractor/client partners. A modular audit will not, by its nature, analyse technical minutiae.

Mid-term intentions are also important when considering an audit. A one-off performance audit is useful in itself, but has effectively nil impact if there is insufficient client-side management time available to manage through any corrective actions. Commissioning a forensic audit with a suspicion that the contract is being managed inappropriately is fine and useful, but will have no effect if the client management is not willing or able to follow through actions that may well be harsh. Part of commissioning any audit of property and property performance is for the client management team to take a strong and realistic view as to how they intend to manage the change and recommendations posed by any auditor.

Finally, the distinctions between types of audit are (hopefully) useful, but are not stringent in any sense. A performance audit may throw up issues where the auditor will recommend a more detailed/forensic examination either during that audit, or at a later date. Most audits — save those where the contractor/client relationship is poor — will contain some elements of a partnering approach: courteous discussions with the contractor about the audit's purpose, presentation of a draft audit report to the contractor before final publication of the findings, for example.

By talking in terms of broad audit categories, we only mean to give a sense of what each entails. Combining approaches — which is far more usual — can provide a mixture of impacts. If a performance audit throws up a major statutory malpractice, the client can rest assured that he will know of it rapidly, and that change will be forced upon the contractor, regardless of how positive any client/contractor relationship might be.

An auditor will always advise you on the type of audit and audit approach, given the context of the particular contract at the time of the audit itself.

5

Audit Techniques

'How do you drive an auditor completely insane? Tie him to a chair,
stand in front of him and fold up a road map the wrong way.'

Introduction

Auditors use many different techniques to answer audit questions posed. These audit techniques are interrelated, and may sound similar at first read. They all have one point in common — used properly, they allow an auditor to see clearly, and to isolate important elements from those more tangential.

Understanding the performance of a contract can be as simple as a checklist of information held by a client — a modular audit in its most rudimentary sense. Undertaking a performance/compliance/VFM audit, or a forensic or one-off audit, however, means being able to understand any audit subject in context, and within a wide variety of parameters.

A knack of auditing is to be able to see the parameters necessary for assessment more or less simultaneously. By rapidly being able to place an audit question in a variety of contexts, any auditor can come to an initial opinion as to whether all might be in order, or not. If not, in this initial view, the techniques described further below provide the guidelines for a detailed assessment of why that might be so, and what the ramifications of any failure truly are.

Audits, by their nature, deal with significant amounts of data as part of any exercise. Auditors will be specialists in their areas, and will have learned how to deal with the huge amounts of detail properly, over time. This chapter, then, shows how we do it.

Overarching Audit Concepts

HOW TO SEE CLEARLY

A given for any auditor commencing an audit is that great subtle and non-subtle attempts are going to be made to blow smoke, deflect and distract the auditor from pursuing his specific aim, or to prevent him from seeing what the audit-subject does not want seen. A great part of auditing skill is to be able to see behind these attempts, as well as deciphering what those attempts mean, in order to see what he wishes to see clearly and in context.

Part of the knack of seeing clearly in any complex audit is to break down all data supplied into components that can be seen clearly. These components can include contractor attempts to hide data, as contributory elements to understanding the data itself.

To expand on these last two points:

- Breaking an audit subject into individual components to understand compliance overall is a critical audit technique. If the subject matter is Health & Safety compliance, as in the diagram that follows illustrates, the only way to determine whether one's FM contractor might be compliant or not, is by looking at each individual element with its individual requirements, and to place findings within the context of the central requirement itself. Attempting to answer the question without the detailed steps is likely to result in generalities, or a misunderstanding of the true facts of compliance.

- Seeing through any contractor's attempt to deflect an audit question is also fundamental. Some aspects of what a contractor might say to an audit question can be useful, if non-valuable to the question itself. Similarly, if a contractor does make great efforts to make data non-available, and dependent on what that data is that is being hidden, a 'fail' response might arrive that much quicker. If, as in the example below, risk assessments are not available or available, but not on site, Health & Safety compliance is automatically unsatisfactory (as risk assessments must be continually available to site personnel, and seen to be so).

The diagram below shows how one breaks down a complex subject into discrete areas of examination. The rationale to the diagram can be used for any other subject, or overall contract performance audit, in that it simply illustrates how a subject matter can be understood by examination of all sub-elements to it.

Audit question: Is our FM contractor compliant with all Health & Safety legislation within his remit?

In terms of understanding clearly if a contract is performing well overall, a similar technique would be used. Here, the contract would be broken down into individual subject areas (service streams, or management regimes), and each broken down into critical and fundamental areas of compliance. Looking at any contract overall means taking this building-block approach and applying it to each and every subject matter. By doing so, an auditor can see clearly the relative import of any area under examination within the context of the whole.

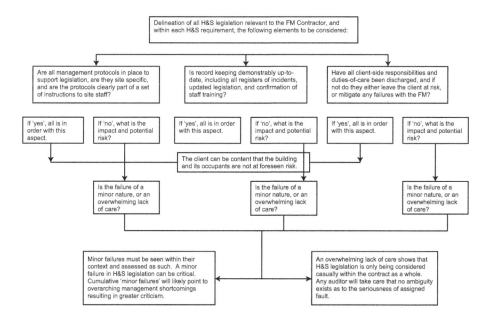

Figure 5.1   An example of how to break down a complex subject into discrete areas of compliance

If we were asked to assess a contract's overall performance level, then, we would:

- isolate the major contractual service streams;

- isolate the major contractual provisions within them;

- be certain that all contributory factors to those contractual provisions were assessed (legislative requirements, or good business practice for example);

- assess each service stream in itself;

- assess each service stream against each other (to look for trends in mismanagement and relative successes/failures);

- assess the weighting of any individual or overall failure within the whole, to determine its import with the context of the contract itself;

- opine on the contract's overall 'health'. (After all of this, an audit team is usually able to score a contractor's performance, informally, in marks out of ten.)

Isolating component parts of any subject matter is one part of seeing an audit subject clearly. For anyone unfamiliar with property auditing though, seeing past contractor distractions is an equal part of understanding compliance.

We knew of one contractor who apparently used to wear a particular red shirt when he knew auditors were expected on site — even if that site visit was to meet with the client team only and with no audits scheduled. This was found out sometime post-audit, and was truthfully thought to be a good ploy by the auditors. The shirt was subtle enough (the auditors never saw it), and it sent a clear message to his team to be on their guard, look busy, and keep any panic attacks to a minimum. The contractor's view, apparently, was that any auditor would make a mental note of anything they saw, however casually, and follow up any potential issue at a later date. (He was right, on the whole, incidentally.)

On another occasion, an audit was stopped in its tracks when the contractor challenged the public-sector's basic right to audit (and this despite the contractual provisions). The contractor argued, successfully for a time, that the public sector could not specifically examine VFM issues except during scheduled benchmarking exercises, and some time was spent correcting that view. The point here is that the contractor did buy time with the ruse, and the subsequent audit challenge was to not let any frustration with the contract management team interfere with determining the truth (rather than any suggestion of punitive findings due to the massive irritation of the audit team).

On the ground, seeing clearly becomes more difficult. Two basic strategies — overwhelming the audit team with paperwork, or frustrating the audit with a paucity of information — will always fail, but will tend to be time-consuming. A contractor will often consider that bombarding an auditor with reams of paper will overwhelm the auditor sufficiently that he will give up — or write only vaguely about how much (unconsidered) evidence there seems to be. The other stratagem, of keeping any data provision to a minimum, is hoped to produce a reaction that much more must be in existence, and is bound to be of good quality (rather than the automatic failure which will always be the audit findings).

Then there are the other individual attempts to deflect/distract an auditor:

- Raising a myriad of subjects other than the one under consideration under the guise of being open and cooperative. If any interest is shown by the auditor, to lead him gently into an examination of the subject the contractor would prefer. Here, assuming that the ploy is seen for what it is, the auditor will become even more curious about the subject originally tabled.

- Confusing formal interview appointments so that the audit team is faced with a fait-accompli of an individual they are not prepared for. Here, the auditor may or may not take what is given, but will, under no circumstances, allow the scheduled interview itself **not** to take place.

- Present data and withdraw it after a time, after finding that more up-to-date information exists. The idea here is that the auditor will become immersed in the 'old' data and find it more difficult to analyse what is purported to be 'true'. Here the auditor will likely allow one or more replacements, but will take note of old and new data, and what it might mean in context. Also, of course, the auditor will draw a line at a time of his own choosing and not allow any further information to be presented.

- Insist continually that what is being asked for is beyond the remit of the audit proper, or beyond the remit of anything they have been asked for before throughout their professional life, so that extracting data is — as the old adage goes — like pulling teeth. Here, depending on the subject, the auditor is likely to rely on client insistence and assistance in carrying out the defined audit.

Whether a contractor tries to obfuscate deliberately (that is, as part of a considered management decision) or not, the idea of trying to deflect an audit team is as old as the hills. In this sense, an audit can be a game of 'cops and robbers', where it is considered (by the contractor) to be fair to use any legal ploy they have to **not** have the auditor come what they came to see. An auditor, to be clear, tends to approach any audit in a similar vein. While an audit team will always enter into an audit situation hoping for the best, and simply trying to do the job they were commissioned for, in the back of any auditor's mind will be 'and what are they trying to hide here, and here and here'.

Contractor ploys aside, the real skill of an auditor therefore is to be able to look at the woods and the trees simultaneously. A contractor ploy can provide useful information in itself, but is unlikely to tip any balance in audit findings. Seeing the woods and the trees here is knowing what the analysis of data shows, looking at what the contractor is trying to hide, and placing both elements squarely within the context of the audit itself, and the contract as a whole.

THE CENTRALITY OF INDEPENDENCE

Any client is likely to have their strong reasons for commissioning a performance audit — and these are likely to go further than their public sector accountability requirements. There may be a need to respond to ministerial queries, or to prepare for a new contract let, or to develop an argument for further funding, or to test whether savings can be made. There may be ongoing suspicions that performance of a service is not as it should be or the management team just becomes tired of hearing complaints from their colleagues.

Clients may believe themselves to be wronged in the functioning of the contract and this is, overall, the point where most audits commence. An auditor is likely to be instructed to confirm/deny that the contract or any individual issue within the contract is functioning as intended. The instruction may include the requirement to look forensically at a subject. The client's perception of the issue may be founded on some experience, and where satisfactory answers to his perceived issues are not being reasonably provided by the contractor.

As an auditor, listening to client's perceptions of the service being provided for them is a natural part of taking any brief. During the audit itself, ignoring those client perceptions is equally fundamental, and so the auditor only relies on the facts presented (hard data) during the exercise.

Given that any consultant, including any auditor, wants to satisfy their client, but that an audit process must be objective and independent, ignoring a client's wishes for any result can be difficult. Situations do arise where a client will make it known that a particular result would suit him (corporately) very well. In these instances, any auditor should be certain he understands his client, and takes trouble to inform him clearly that the audit will only have value if the desired result can be seen to be true, demonstrably, in fact. In the highly unusual circumstance of a client insisting on a particular result, and those results cannot be seen in fact, any auditor will have no choice but to formally disagree and resign.

Circumstances are entirely rare, in our experience, where any great attempt to sway a result is made — on the public sector side at least. An auditor's credibility is always bound up with any audit he undertakes, and any auditor will know that it is better to not undertake any kind of audit, rather than to undertake it dishonestly (to skew a result).

Having said that, examples of where client perceptions might be introduced into an audit instruction might be as in the following examples (to broadly illustrate, hypothetically):

- The client has repeatedly asked for substantiating information on a Forward Works Programme (FWP), and these requests have been minuted. The contractor continuously assures the client that all is in order, but finds that ongoing management issues make it impossible to provide the complete information desired. The client is feeling entirely frustrated in insisting on the Plan's provision, and finds he cannot readily directly insist on its provision by a certain date (this, the client feels, would be using a sledgehammer too quickly for a single contractual fault). Here, the client may ask his auditor to understand any issues surrounding the curation and provision of a Forward Works Programme in its entirety, and to quote 'chapter and verse' on its existence as an industry standard document, or not.

Any auditor here understands that his client is frustrated by misleading and contradictory information. He understands that a sub-text of this client perception might be an interest in finding that the contractor has breached his contractual terms. An FWP is a technical document that should be curated according to many industry guidelines for doing so, and it will either exist as that robust description of forward works, or not. Also, the auditor will look at what factual statements were made by the contractor in its provision, and compare dates of when statements were made against the state of the FWP at that time. Any auditor will take a negative view on any contractor who has misstated the truth, if it were found, for example, that an FWP did not factually exist at the time where unequivocal statements were made that it did.

Contrarily, there are occasions where the client could be found to be a contributory factor to this FWP's non-existence. An auditor will want to know if the contractor can demonstrate that client fault exists. This hypothetical client fault might be through a lack of response for guidance on the document's curation, an agreement to waive its production to an unspecified future date, or through non-release of critical information (even though requested).

This example shows where a client has used an audit to formally assist him in receiving a document required, without having to formally insist through legal means or further disproportionate management steps. Here, the client has used his knowledge that all was not well with the document's provision to seek further assurances about its potential quality overall. For an audit team, looking to discover the truth of a contractor statement is bread-and-butter work, and a client perception of any contractor fault is entirely incidental to answering the question.

Another example might be the following:

- The client has received repeated complaints from his Minister's office that catering is slow, and this has caused embarrassment at governmental meetings. As the client has not received other complaints on the service, he may ask an auditor to look at catering provision as a whole, and with a specific examination of Ministerial-level service provision. The client here wishes to be able to clearly say to his Minister exactly what the level of service is, and what steps have been taken to resolve his concerns.

This exercise would be heavily dependent on the accuracy of Helpdesk records, and internal management protocols for delivery of soft services. The auditor would check catering requests by the Minister's office and compare them against any signed receipt for their provision. The data would be compared against the specific contractual requirement (in terms of any maximum time for provision allowable, and the minimum amount of time necessary for the contractor to prepare catering for any single event) and the complaints themselves. If the contractor were found to be operating within the terms of the contract, there would be nothing to say in terms of compliance. If, however, the contractor was consistently operating at the fringes of compliance — as in, delivery of catering being on the edge of any allowable time-frame — the auditor might recommend the FM management team recommends to the contractor that he takes more care in satisfying their contractual requirements more 'wholeheartedly'.

Here too, the auditor would take care that catering requests were reasonable, and within the boundaries of any contractual requirements/cut-off points for catering provision. Before making any accusation of contractor fault, the auditor would want to be assured that their client was without blame. It might be, for example, that the service provision was timely, and the sense of any catering being unduly delayed was simply a perception and one that can be easily corrected by showing those concerned why that is so.

Here, the client might need to be quietly corrected on his perceptions and the report itself used to neutrally explain the reality of service delivery.

Being practical, though, there is no harm in listening to any detail of any client's concern, and to use it to help inform the audit brief, and the audit itself. Given that any audit will be conducted transparently, taking a steer from a client where they might feel a true issue is lurking in one particular spot, and looking at that as one would any other issue, is completely legitimate.

We have known instances where a client's perceptions of a hidden problem have been entirely with and without foundation. The point here is that while there might be a vested interest in a client trying to steer an audit — and steer is too strong a word really — any auditor will treat such a request as he would from any source. The auditor will naturally think 'that's interesting', and look at the issue identified in the detail that is appropriate to the subject.

Most contractors will try to influence an auditor if they can, and for all understandable reasons. This influence is likely to be through some kind of a charm offensive, and the straightforward business arguments that he knows the auditor is likely to understand. Any contractor will feel it is worth some time trying to have the auditor see his point of view clearly — that his business is being conducted in difficult contractual and corporate circumstances, and that any faults are not of his making but due to circumstances largely beyond his control.

We knew of one circumstance where the attempt to influence findings was more overt. The contractor pleaded that he had inherited circumstances which were untenable, and so he could not ultimately be held responsible for any failures found under his remit. The contractual arguments were easy to dismiss, for any number of reasons. The auditor went a further step in demonstrating his independence from the results the contractor wished to influence — by refusing the contractor's offer to go out for coffee so to demonstrate the formality of the audit.

Here, given that the contractor was completely at sea in his running of his contract, and appeared to have little knowledge of how the public sector needs to do its business — transparently — the auditor felt that a fairly dramatic gesture should be made to illustrate the point. By refusing an innocuous cup of coffee, the auditor then took pains to say why he did so. The auditor wanted the contractor to know that there was no likelihood of his being able to say he influenced the report.

Vested interests, therefore, can be overcome in three ways:

- by insistence on the independence of any audit as a fundamental precept at the time of any audit commission;

- by seeing any wished-for-result in its context to determine its veracity with clarity, based on hard data;

- by physically removing oneself from any situation that could even remotely be seen as compromising.

The central precepts of a successful audit always remain, and influence every aspect of its conduct: audits must be conducted openly and independently, so that opinions made can be fully justified. All other aspects to the audit process remain based on those two facts.

TRANSPARENCY OF DATA AND OF THE AUDIT PROCESS

Auditors talk a lot about transparency, both of data and of process. Transparency, to an auditor, means that any subject under consideration is clear and reasoned, with all steps to and around the subject clearly able to be seen. The concept of transparency was defined above, and this section provides more detailed technical information.

Transparency of data and processes

In terms of auditing proper, a transparent piece of data is where it is possible to clearly see where that datum fits into the process as a whole. Transparency of process is where there is a clear visible connection between pieces of data, between management processes, and where all are clearly constructed to satisfy the contract and other public sector/industry concerns.

To illustrate:

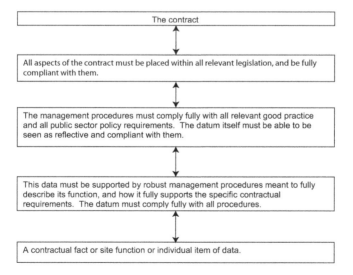

Figure 5.2   Illustration of levels of transparency within a contract

If we were an FM Contractor looking to (at least partially) satisfy an auditor as to his management systems, we would spend some time ensuring that our processes were visible and reasoned. The FM Contractor should be fully aware that auditors get worried when they cannot see clearly why something was done, or to what end. Auditors get more worried when no one can explain a process or a function. To an auditor, if an FM manager is not fully aware of his own accountability requirements (through transparency of processes and actions), then that contract is likely to be in some difficulty from the start.

To explain a bit further — auditors will assume that any corporate action has meaning within the contract itself. In public sector contracts, part of understanding if funding is spent well is ensuring that any contractor can demonstrate that his systems are strong, and incapable of systematic misuse. If a contract has processes that are hidden — that is, it is not able to be seen what actions might take place between the start and finish of a process — any auditor will have some disquiet.

An easy example here is through any small works procurement in an FM Contract. If a works project costs £10,000 (payable to the FM Contractor) part of the transparency of the process will be in understanding how that sum was built up. If a contractor here cannot show the detail of the overall cost build up, any auditor will have some disquiet as to potential disproportionate profitability for the FM Contractor, or inappropriate management fees being charged on for sub-contractors (as in, double, or triple).

Another example might be in training. If central management records show that all staff are appropriately trained for their site tasks, but no local or specific records exist showing that staff did in fact receive that training, an auditor is likely to question whether or not that training did take place.

Knowing this, FM contractors can do a great deal to prepare for any audit. A rough guide to how an auditor might begin to understand if any process is transparent is:

- Is the contract Quality Management system up-to-date and ISO accredited?

- Do existing site processes fully reflect those requirements without deviations?

If the answer to either of the two questions is 'no', a contractor should know that an auditor is likely to find difficulties with his systems, and that more difficulties will likely arise.

The interdependence of record keeping/site performance is discussed later as another discrete sub-section. Transparency, however, is about being able to simply see management actions and processes as clear demonstrations of their part in the fulfilment of the contract.

Transparency of the audit itself

But transparency requirements are equally applicable to the conduct of an audit itself. Given that audits can be controversial, in terms of expressing unwelcome opinions, it is of fundamental importance that an auditor can demonstrate very clearly why any element of the process was undertaken as it was, and so how any opinions were formed.

The diagram below illustrates the steps that should be shown to clearly demonstrate the audits process itself.

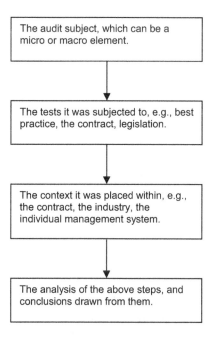

Figure 5.3   **Illustration of the transparency of the audit process**

Once upon a time, a long long time ago, an auditor was instructed to comment in the broadest possible terms as to whether or not a contract was functioning as intended. The client here had concerns about varied staffing issues, and he wished to be able to alleviate senior client-side management concerns about overstaffing, and (above all) why the perception continued to exist that the contract was failing.

The auditor here used various techniques to answer the question, including shadowing management staff, real-time problem-solving situations, and formal and informal interviews with all concerned (contractor and client-side). While some data analysed was therefore fairly soft, the audit proved to be successful because every opinion was fully justified by the way an opinion was founded. By quoting the methodology, and outlining the specific steps taken to arrive at the conclusion, the audit did result in management change.

The point here is that any auditor must be able to fully justify any sentence, or qualifying or definitive language to all and sundry, and without that ability any audit will not stand.

Transparency of the audit process tends to be easier than the example quoted above. For example, an audit norm is to look at percentages of data in order to form opinions of the subject as a whole.

If, as a totally hypothetical example, there might be 100 reactive maintenance tasks in any one month, an auditor will choose up front (that is, pre-audit), to examine 10–15 per cent of those tasks, randomly chosen. If the reactive task numbers increase hugely to, say, 2,000, the auditor will feel that a 10 per cent sampling is too great and unnecessary in order to see the subject clearly using this technique, and will look at a smaller percentage. An auditor will choose his percentage to be sampled on the basis of achieving a meaningful result, without broadening it so much as to make the sampling redundant (as in, if a high percentage of sampling records are chosen to be examined, the subject might best be examined using another audit technique).

In terms of transparency, with this technique, declaring the percentage sampled makes the results of the analysis clear and beyond dispute (in those terms). If an auditor declares the likelihood of a broad failure, and says that the reasoning for declaring that failure is because of a high level of non-compliance in the chosen sample, an FM contractor can only request broadening the sample, or accepting the results. By using proportionate sampling, the audit process

— and the results from it — are clear as all data, including the methods of its collection are demonstrable, and any other person should be able to examine the records and come to the same conclusion.

However, it is important to note that if any result of the sampling shows a heavy failure percentage, the audit is likely to show great concern and recommend a more detailed examination to ascertain definitively if the failure is 'real', or just a bad random draw of tasks. In practice, during a site audit, if the sampled records show wholly consistent passes or fails, any auditor is likely to pick another few random records to confirm/deny the apparent result. If the failure rate remains high, the audit is likely to recommend a more wholesale examination of the issue under consideration to determine definitively the result, through the use of other audit techniques.

Other techniques, such as looking at a management regime for one service, and extrapolating its key points to make reasonable observations on the likelihood of recurrence in other service streams, are also clear and a valid audit methodology. Here an auditor will take care to comment only on the service examined, form any overall opinions through processes that are seen to be applicable to other service streams (Quality Management systems, procurement, training and so on) and substantiate the point through a brief sampling of systems to ensure that a parallel does exist.

What is less clear, and unsustainable, is for an auditor to go into any audit without a clear methodology for its construct. While a variety of techniques can and will be used, undoubtedly, it is fatal for any audit to be constructed without due deliberation and without the full realisation that the audit findings themselves are open to full transparency and detailed discussion.

Standing back from this — for any public sector body looking to commission an audit, transparency of process is nothing to be particularly concerned about at the time of its commission. Looking at any audit result, however, any public sector body should be able to see clearly how any opinions were arrived at, through the auditors careful description of the transparent steps undertaken — or transparency/lack of transparency of any contractor data in the audit itself. Understanding how auditors view transparency, therefore, is to be able to see their workings clearly and how transparency of contractor data is an important contributory factor.

HOW AN AUDITOR CAN SEE CLEARLY OVER TIME

Any auditor worth his salt will always only see what is put in front of him, and examine any issue only in the context of best practice, the contract, and all other relevant framework concepts and strategies. Any auditor will always discount anecdotal evidence until proven by verifiable data, and will always discount any attempts to sway an opinion, unless similarly justified. This book talks about the independence of auditing throughout its pages.

However, situations can arise where a team of auditors audit one contract consistently over its tenure. In this example, the auditors will have somewhere in the back of their minds previous findings, previous (unsupported) opinions that were therefore never published and so on. Having that knowledge assists, on the whole, for long-term work, as the memory of those previous findings, suspicions and opinions will allow for better contextualisation, and allows them to avoid rediscovering any contractual wheel.

Having the knack of knowing detailed history, and yet only commenting on the findings of the time, is a skill gained over years of audit work. And still, in these circumstances, knowing that, say, an identical problem was uncovered some time ago, or in a previous management regime, brings a valuable perspective to any issue under discussion. It's a question of nuance, and of careful weighting to ensure that any one perspective — historic knowledge versus current findings — is not overemphasised unduly to the detriment of an accurate audit report.

Any audit team leader in these circumstances will instruct his audit team to discount any previous knowledge during the audit itself. In the run-up to any audit for CLG, for example, we have taken care to remind ourselves of any issues we have examined previously, and to remind ourselves of our formal recommendations. This knowledge does form a base for the forthcoming audit, as it provides a loose framework for where we might look next.

During the audit itself, though, the audit team will be clearly instructed, and overseen to be certain it is so, to keep an open mind as to what they might see. It could be, for example, that the FM Contractor has found a different solution to the problem identified. It could be that other more important management priorities have taken precedence, and that these changing priorities are found to be valid in the context of the whole. On the other hand, the contractor may have deliberately taken no action, or have continued to misunderstand/mis-provide the service under examination.

It is a question of nuance.

For example (and these are purely hypothetical):

- A previous audit showed loose management of minor works procurement. Previous findings showed that, while no suspicion of malpractice (fraud) was held by the audit team, the management framework was sufficiently weak to allow for inappropriate procurement to take place. In the new exercise, the audit team would have a mental aide-memoire to see if the arrangements had been altered to take into account recommendations, but would only comment on the arrangements as found. If the auditor found that systems had weakened further, he is likely to make a more direct criticism of the existing arrangements, point to the period of time where the opportunity did allow for improvement, and make current recommendations more stringent.

- In the conduct of a previous audit, various rumours abounded about cleaning service provision, and where staffing levels were felt to be inappropriate for the tasks. Part of the current audit remit is to look at cleaning staffing levels, and the auditor recalls those rumours. Here, however, and unlike the previous example, the auditor would place no weight on historic rumours in his findings, but simply look at data presented because those rumours would have been impossible to prove regardless.

- A previous audit found evidence of a lax management regime and recommended corrective action. The new audit finds that no action has been taken, the contractor citing intrusive audit requirements as a justification for non-action. Here, the audit would take a harsh view on lack of action, as the previous report had been explicitly accepted by the contractor. The previous audit's work would be a valid report to comment/compare against given the seeming intransigence of the contractor.

Contextualisation of Audit Subjects

MICRO TO MACRO AND VERTICAL AND HORIZONTAL AUDITING

Independence, an enquiring mind, personality traits, audit strategies, and detailed specialist knowledge are primary elements in the successful conduct of any performance/VFM audit. Of equal importance in choosing an audit team is having auditors who can look at macro-micro contract elements and trace any detail horizontally or vertically with ease. Doing so means that any element of any part of any audit can be placed with its appropriate weight within the audit findings and the contract itself. This is a specialist skill that can only be learned over time.

Any auditor needs to be able to read and skim read large amounts of data very quickly, and retain that data sufficiently to be able to place it in its appropriate context — an auditor must be a speed-reader. An auditor needs to have an innate practicality about him. This practicality will help inform the speed-reading, so that data can be seen easily for what it is (simple meaningless management verbiage, or inherently pointing out a contractual deviation, for example).

But the 'knack' of micro-macro/vertical-horizontal examination goes further than practical (learned) skills, and has its cornerstone with a deep and detailed understanding of facilities management contracts and public sector accountability requirements. This is to say that in order to understand if a fault is a major or minor one, any auditor will need to understand the significance of an issue within a series of contexts, simultaneously:

- Best Practice

- Public Sector Accountability Requirements and all other Public Sector policy mandates

- Industry Specialisms

- The specific contract.

What any audit team does, in practice, is to take any one piece of data, and look at that data for meaning in itself, then place that data within the overarching contexts identified above. This is to say that an auditor will consider the individual failure as a simple piece of information and understand its import within its subject area, before placing it in the context of best practice/contractual requirements and so on. The auditor, in order to determine if any error is important, can only do so by understanding if the failure is relatively meaningless within its context, or has the potential of causing a greater effect (by transgressing an important statute, or through knock-on effects to the building's management).

The only way to understand any individual issue in any property audit of whatever type is through this detailed knowledge. One can only know if one component failure represents a critical failure, or not, by a thorough understanding of its significance within the whole.

The diagram above on 'transparency of process' illustrates the various contexts that a micro/macro /horizontal/vertical audit would be placed within. The diagrams below show visually the two techniques for further assessing an audit subject.

To illustrate further:

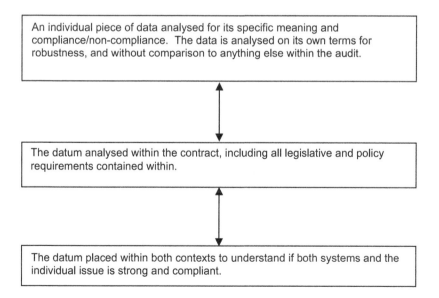

Figure 5.4   The structure of a micro/macro audit

And to discuss:

FIRST STEP

If we take our piece of datum to be a Helpdesk record, we would understand that record for its own meaning. We would examine things like:

- Is the datum itself likely to be true in technological terms — how has the record been entered into the Helpdesk system, and is the information input sufficient to describe the datum in the detail required?

- Does the datum itself fulfil the contractual requirement — was it timely, accurate and meaningful?

- Is the datum open to manipulation at Helpdesk or in the site operation that produced it?

- Can the site operation itself be seen to be as described — were there any complaints, or evidence of supervisory checks?

SECOND STEP

We would then take the same piece of data and put it into a wider context of contractual compliance. We would examine things like:

- Has the datum clearly fulfilled all applicable best practice, legislative, statutory and local policy requirements?

- How can compliance with any of these mandates be proven? Are the records demonstrating compliance up-to-date, non-generic and directly applicable to the site operation?

- Has the site operation that produced the datum fulfilled any wider contractual mandates relevant to it — does it demonstrate VFM, adherence to a contract plan, reflect environmental targets?

THIRD STEP

We would then look at the same piece of datum in both contexts. We would examine things like:

- Is there a clear and demonstrable connection between the piece of datum and overarching management structures?

- Is management attention being paid to consider the site operation/ datum within any wider contractual policy and business concerns (VFM and so on)?

- How does this one piece of datum compare to the others likely examined as part of this sampling exercise? If there are differences, why? Do comparisons between the whole show a clear trend of issues at any level of the process?

- What does this analysis tell us at a micro (datum) level and at an operational macro level? Is there any fault specifically or generally, or are all systems strong and fulfilling the contractual requirement?

A horizontal/vertical audit has similar processes:

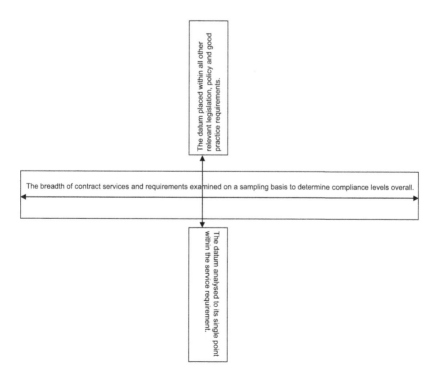

Figure 5.5   The structure of a horizontal/vertical audit

A horizontal/vertical audit provides a different way of assessing context. An audit using these techniques can start either vertically or horizontally.

In a horizontal audit we would undertake a sampling check of the area to be examined across all aspects of its provision. The area to be examined could be the functioning of the contract as a whole, or a discrete service area. To use a specific example, however, we would, in the case of Helpdesk functioning examine things like:

- How does the Helpdesk function overall — is the software of good quality, are the data entry fields open to manipulation after entry, are the Helpdesk operators appropriately trained for their task?

- How are requests received — by phone, email and intranet? In each of these instances, what happens when there is any backlog of tasks, and how can these tasks themselves known to be accurate in those circumstances?

- Is the Helpdesk data founded on accurate base data — are floor plans up-to-date, is any condition survey (which will form the base for an asset register, and therefore PPM system) within industry standards, how does the Helpdesk deal with variations in personnel and contact details?

- How does the functioning of the Helpdesk fit within the overall contractual requirement — does it fulfil the contract's specific requirements for its functioning?

- How are the records analysed to report on overall compliance in the Helpdesk functioning itself, and individual service stream performance? Is the reportage system robust, and readily seen to be accurate?

In a vertical audit on the same subject, we would:

- Sample individual Helpdesk records to test their compliance with the service itself — can PPM records be seen to be accurate, can the complaints register be certain to sweep up all customer complaints?

- How does the contractor know that services are being provided as stated on the Helpdesk records? What sample checks are being made to ensure quality of work?

- Do those individual records reflect compliance with the individual service stream requirements? Do the sample records largely demonstrate the fulfilment of any requirements for statutory compliance or timeliness or assurance of quality?

- Do the records demonstrate compliance with the local contract plan/quality assurance system? How does the contractor assure the robustness of his management procedures at a micro and macro level?

As further examples of how an auditor would understand the proper context of an issue using either of the techniques described above:

- PPM record keeping is found to be somewhat lax. The auditor has no particular comment to make on whether or not PPM is physically carried out on schedule, as signatures for job sheets are in place, and he notes that job sheets are printed off and distributed as one would expect. However, the signed job sheets (signifying that works have taken place) are simply filed, and no notice is seemingly taken of any parts replacements that have occurred, or other observations on the condition of the plant recently maintained.

  - The auditor then thinks two things: should some management view be taken of the PPM job sheets so that any necessary updating of the building's asset register can occur, and; should some management view be taken of the results of PPM as a whole (and so that contractor management can continuously consider the ratio of planned versus reactive maintenance over all, through trend analysis)?

    Here, hypothetically, the auditor would consider the small break in a robust management chain of plant maintenance to be of reasonable significance. His opinion would likely be that the system should be altered immediately, and that the client team is at some risk until it is done. A robust asset register is paramount for understanding future capital costs, and this asset register cannot be seen to be complete without incorporating appropriate PPM records.

- Training records for contractor site staff are difficult to understand, and appear contradictory. The auditor has been presented with different versions of staff training records which are difficult to reconcile, leading him to mistrust the records as a whole. No clear explanation is given as to why that is so, and the auditor is unable to answer the basic question of 'are site staff appropriately trained for their role'?

  Hypothetically here, the auditor would consider that the contractor is at substantial risk from breaching Health & Safety Regulations, and will inform the client that they are now at risk too (having understood that H&S training is probably incomplete from the time of their reading of the audit report). The client will now have a duty of care to see that training is up-to-date, and will need to see that it is done. The contractor would have failed on multiple levels — through potentially providing personnel to function in and manage a building without having the training to do so (and this will be a breach of contract, as well as applicable H&S legislation). This simple lack of explicatory paperwork would be seen as a serious failure.

In both instances, an apparently minor laxity in paperwork effectively has a potentially greater ramification than it would appear. The auditor knows this, because he understands H&S regulations, and understands how a robust PPM system is a foundation of asset maintenance.

A converse view is when an apparently major breach is fairly meaningless in terms of the operation of the contract as a whole. In practice, these 'apparently major breaches which prove to be fairly meaningless' are found to be so because management action has immediately taken place to correct the situation, the breach is a 'one-off', or because of human error.

For example:

- Receptionists are not on duty when the auditor arrives. The auditor knows that this should never ever happen, and would want to know why that has occurred. However, the auditor also notes that security guards are in attendance, and that (by trying) he cannot enter the building without a proper pass/escort. A receptionist turns up five minutes later, and the auditor duly enters.

Here, hypothetically, the contractor has failed, but the auditor would likely only take passing note of the problem he witnessed, unless further enquiries showed clearly that this was a regular ongoing issue. As the building remained secured, the isolated failure (which occurred because of human error) is not worth considering. If no security guards had been in attendance, obviously, the auditor would have been radically more concerned.

And then, placing any individual failure, or numbers of failures, within an audit result as a whole is also a necessity. When does a micro failure result in a stinging critique about performance as a whole, and when does it not?

In the examples above, if the audit subject is simply to look at engineering, the individual failure to take account of completed PPM records would still be treated as significant, even if other aspects of engineering appeared to be in order. Robust record keeping is a particular requirement of a number of H&S regulations, and non-compliance here could also mean a breach of H&S legislation. An auditor would take the view that, even if other engineering records can be seen to be robust, failures will be inherent through the lack of incorporation of PPM findings. Similarly, with the training example, any auditor will take any possible breach of H&S requirements as worthy of a strong headline in the report's Executive Summary. With inadequate training records, the auditor will know that his client is at risk until site staff are appropriately trained, or face implication within H&S legislation should an accident occur.

Conversely, the missing receptionist — while minor in itself, as a one-off — could readily be seen by an auditor to be significant if receptionist/security staff overall are understaffed. Here, the auditor might recommend that the client determines if sufficient numbers of staff are properly employed by the contractor, and within the context of the contractor's original tender return.

SUMMARY

Micro-macro/horizontal-vertical auditing structures are both meant to see any audit subject in its proper context.

Micro-macro auditing takes an individual datum, and then traces it up — step-by-step — to its proper place within the contractual construct.

Vertical-horizontal auditing is meant as a shorthand to indicate either a:

* sampling check across a range of services (a horizontal examination), or

* a detailed analysis of one service, or individual datum, within all business and contractual requirements that apply to it (a vertical examination).

Audits will always use versions of these structures to determine a factual context for success/failure. The point of working within the audit techniques is to make the context for audit opinions as valid and clear as possible. Seeing an audit datum as an isolated fact does not necessarily show its overall success/ failure. Looking at a contract broadly, does not necessarily accurately describe any individual problems.

Using the two structures together will always provide a more realistic context for assessment.

SYSTEMS VERSUS THE ACTUALITY OF SITE PERFORMANCE

Part of any auditors understanding of context also relies on a clear knowledge of the relative importance of managerial and operational systems versus the actuality of performance. These two simple interdependent concepts provide another framework for a successful audit.

A strong up-to-date ISO 9001 accredited management system will not necessarily describe the adequacy of site delivery. An immaculate building without the means to describe how that has been performed provides no means of analysing how that has been achieved. The obvious point is that management systems and on-the-ground delivery must work together seamlessly and in harmony.

The diagram opposite illustrates the point.

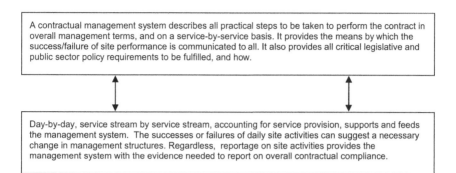

A contractual management system describes all practical steps to be taken to perform the contract in overall management terms, and on a service-by-service basis. It provides the means by which the success/failure of site performance is communicated to all. It also provides all critical legislative and public sector policy requirements to be fulfilled, and how.

Day-by-day, service stream by service stream, accounting for service provision, supports and feeds the management system. The successes or failures of daily site activities can suggest a necessary change in management structures. Regardless, reportage on site activities provides the management system with the evidence needed to report on overall contractual compliance.

Figure 5.6   The interrelationship between management systems and site performance

Management systems

A management/operational system is a skeleton from which all practical site activities take place — the site performance of any one contract. The management systems should clearly reflect contractual requirements, and provide the route map for all site staff to fulfil their duties. Without strong management systems, the contract can only be practically executed in a series of isolated voids. Internal understandings of the contract's success/failure will be impossible to demonstrate, and the contractor will find it impossible to manage the contract as a whole.

Management and operational systems are generally undertaken in the context of Quality Assurance procedures, and to fulfil a contractual requirement to have a Contract Plan (or some similar construct). Management systems can be examined as a discrete part of contract compliance, or as a tool to understand if site compliance is as expected by that plan, or as a referral document to guide an auditor through the kinds of information he might expect when examining an individual service within any contract.

Auditors tend to be interested in both management systems and execution, even with the simplest and most straightforward of audit tasks. A management system should clearly describe for an auditor what he should be looking for in terms of data collection and daily tasks, and should clearly reflect what any individual FM Contract might say on the subject.

For example:

A client has questions about his FM Contractor's security service provision, and commissions an audit to confirm if all security arrangements are strong and do not expose the building's occupants to any risk. All FM Contracts are likely to describe how this security service should be conducted, but these descriptions are likely to be quite broad — as performance specifications are by far the norm (these days).

Given that the contract specification is likely to say something like (in abbreviated form here): 'Keep the buildings secure and safe between 24 hours per day, 365 days per year, through regular patrols, CCTV monitoring, and attendance at reception' any auditor will look to a contractor's management system to understand how the contractor has chosen to expand the bare requirement to an operational guide.

The auditor will expect to see details of record keeping, the ways and means of entry pass production, CCTV monitoring requirements (including their compliance with relevant legislation), length and regularity of patrols and so on.

The auditor will take a view on the systems themselves. He will look at things like:

- When were the operational documents produced (are they out of date)?

- Do they clearly reflect the particular contract's service requirement (are they contract specific, rather than generic)?

- Is there any indication of issuance to site staff (or have they been written to satisfy the contract, and then parked)?

- Do the systems mesh together (is a report produced that is clearly not read or analysed, or do patrolling guards keep no records at all of any observances — even though comment is made elsewhere to client on their success)?

- Are the systems themselves compliant with any ISO accreditation held, and do they adequately reflect applicable legislation (as in, has someone thought about the importance of compliance in this area)?

The auditor will then look at the various site records themselves to understand two things:

- Do the site records reflect the management system (that is, do the site records reflect and comply with their own internal management requirements)?

- Do the records accurately reflect the service provision (as in, notwithstanding the management records, is the building likely to be secure)?

The understanding of management systems, therefore, is not an abstract exercise, but is a confirmation that actions have taken place in a prescribed environment that satisfies all contractual requirements.

Site performance

The truth is that it is difficult, on the whole, for any auditor to understand site performance in any sort of live sense. The understanding of whether, say, hospitality provision is a success or not on the ground would depend on looking at caterers deliver teas and coffees over a period of time, and sample check with end-users to see if they are content with quality, timeliness, friendliness of staff and so on. The greatest understanding any auditor is likely to gain — in this instance — is through analysis of complaints, late deliveries, and refusal to pay invoices.

The paper exercises described provide good bedrock information as to the reality of site performance. Paper exercises are limited though, for several reasons:

- Data can be manipulated to skew results. Paper records will not necessarily reflect what is on the ground — that is, the building might be dirty, while the records say they should be clean or vice versa.

- The answers swept up in any management system might not clearly answer the audit question posed — it might be too general, or not consider an aspect of performance.

- Understanding what the management records show in detail might be disproportionate to any audit question, and so not readily recommended by any auditor.

As examples:

- It takes a particular mindset to formally complain, and so records might show that customer satisfaction is high because of the lack of complaints made. General disgruntlement with any service provision, which could be pervasive, might not be recorded in any complaints register. Further, it will be virtually impossible to know if all complaints are picked up on any FM complaints register. A comment made by a customer to an FM Helpdesk that reports 'disappointment' might not be treated as a formal complaint when it is, really.

- Analysing the minutiae of timings in any service is likely to be a large exercise, and could be disproportionate to the question being asked. If complaints are consistently made that items are late, undertaking this exercise is the only way of knowing if the complaints are valid or not. Attempting to understand any site performance issue solely by tracking requested/received records will in itself only paint a distorted picture of the services overall success/failure (because they will not show any qualitative issues).

The success of using records to correctly identify the adequacy of site performance can most easily used in a matrix, where a record is cross-checked against another facet of delivery. Practically, this strategy would be undertaken on a sampling basis. If any substantial failures were found in that sample, a wider sampling would be undertaken to confirm the results found.

For example, see Figure 5.7.

Shadowing site staff, in the example quoted elsewhere, can be a useful tool for understanding contractor's day-to-day lives. Real-time problem-solving situations are very effective if planned and executed well. Stealthy recorded spying can, in some circumstances, show up aspects of real-time site management that belie management protocols and statements of compliance made.

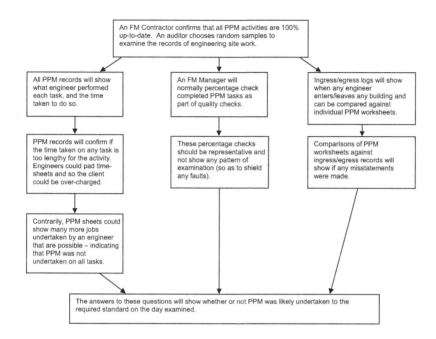

Figure 5.7   Illustration of how an examination of records can accurately demonstrate performance/non-performance

Real time problem-solving must be constructed to be as close to an event that genuinely could occur as possible and must be conducted with a client's close involvement. For example:

- A call could be made to an FM Helpdesk notifying the operator of an H&S emergency and requesting immediate attendance. How long does it take for an appropriate person to arrive?

- A person sits in a building reception area clearly taking note of what is seen, and photographing entrances/exits. How long does it take for the person to be challenged and evicted?

- A clearly irate building user rings the FM Helpdesk to complain. Is the complaint dealt with appropriately, and is the complaint logged in subsequent reportage?

Given that any auditor only spends limited time in any building being examined, real-time problem-solving situations can give a more realistic view of site performance. If problems set are carefully constructed, and subjects chosen to be of maximum relevance to the service under consideration, general (caveated) opinions can be extrapolated about the likelihood (or not) of that individual failure representing a wider management issue.

The interdependence of systems analysis and site performance

If the examination of management records can't do this one thing — to understand clearly how any service might be performing in truth, on the ground, in any one day — they can provide an assessment of the likelihood of this success or failure. On the other hand, while testing of site performance might show that all appears to be in order, management systems might not be able to clearly track results, or paint a distorted picture of the site reality.

While a brief discussion of Key Performance Indicators (KPIs) occurs elsewhere in this book, examining management system records overall and their corollary (evidence to support their implementation on site) will show if those KPIs are in truth being met.

As a hypothetical example here:

- KPIs consistently show that no security breaches take place.

- The contractor consistently shows a 100 per cent success rate in that service provision.

However, examination of site records shows that there is a growing number of unreturned entrance passes. Here, somehow, the contractor should have given some notification that unsecured entrance passes are in existence, and show clearly the steps taken to reduce the occurrence of individuals leaving with passes.

Taking it a step further, any client could arrange for a breach/breaches to take place, one way or another, and wait to see if those breaches were discovered and reflected in subsequent analysis. Here, if the breaches were not noticed, or not notified, the client could be certain that flaws exist in both site management and reportage against targets/contractual requirements. Given that the breaches were likely to be recorded on CCTV, demonstrating their accuracy is a simple task. Understanding why the breach might not be recorded could show relatively minor fault (a one-off oversight) or a major management flaw (the Helpdesk does not sweep up incidents of breaches despite their provision by security staff).

As another example:

- KPIs consistently show that all PPM is being undertaken according to schedule.

- The contractor consistently shows that a 100 per cent success rate in that service provision.

However, and the example is quoted elsewhere, no note is being taken of the results of engineering visits. Here, while the PPM statement might be true, there is no way of proving its accuracy, and PPM might be failing to achieve its overall aim of maximising the lifespan of plant in the building.

Taking it a step further again, any client could choose to spot check individual PPM tasks which will physically reflect attendance — a replacement, or a repair which will show clearly attendance/non-attendance. If, even though records do show that an action did take place on a certain day, but levels of dust (for example) show no signs of anyone physically being able to do the task without its disturbance, would disprove the point.

Examining KPI statements against site records, therefore, is another way of understanding the truth of performance. Spot checks of conformity, if carefully conducted, can readily assist in understanding if reportage is accurate or not.

Another example here might be a contractor held complaints register.

Here:

- The contractor is required to report numbers of complaints on a monthly basis.

- Complaints can be made by email or telephone to the FM Helpdesk, but all complaints must be recorded in a bespoke register.

Examination of overall Helpdesk emails/records of customer calls could show, however, that complaints were being made but not logged as such (and therefore stating contractor more positively than is truthful). The fault here could be the contractor management system, or insufficiently clear requests of staff to make their complaints clearly such, or individual staff negligence. This examination would show more clearly any divergences in (effectively) contractor self-certification of the adequacy of their performance.

As with the examples above, deliberate client complaints made in a variety of circumstances could assist in proving/disproving the accuracy of any complaints register. Any real-time test of this kind, if properly recorded, will provide a strong indication of the likelihood of overarching management or site fault.

In its broadest sense, if an auditor finds that management records are out-of-date, or are generic, or do not describe how they understand their own compliance with the contract, that auditor will feel that the contract is likely to be — more or less — operating in some kind of management void.

Systems are not everything to an auditor, but they do provide an important aspect to a full understanding of a contract's performance. In a VFM/performance audit, management records would be considered as of equal importance to site performance. In a forensic audit, management records would be used as a cornerstone to understanding detailed compliance with the subject concerned. In a partnering audit, management records would be used as a means to assist the contractor in understanding how his systems work in practice. In a modular audit, holding up-to-date records is a broad cornerstone of compliance within that audit structure.

SEEING IN THE ROUND

Performance auditors will regularly talk about the necessity of seeing any issue 'in the round'. In the context of a site audit, the technique of seeing any subject in the round does assist in seeing what the contractor might be attempting to hide, or will show extenuating circumstances which should be considered to mitigate any fault found.

Though it is a question of nuance, seeing a subject 'in the round' differs from a macro/micro or vertical/horizontal examination, in that it also looks at all other extraneous influences on an issue.

These extraneous influences can include elements such as:

- all private sector corporate mandates and constraints (being subject to a takeover, for example, where new management regimes affecting the business as a whole will take a period of time to be fully operational);

- all public sector changes in personnel, or changes in legislation, or in government all of which involve a natural period of management flux;

- the overall state of the contract — how many years it has left to run, a change in KPI calculation as examples.

Seeing any subject 'in the round' looks at the contract overall, rather than a component view of any issue simply within the letter of the contract itself.

To illustrate how mitigating circumstances could qualify any audit opinion:

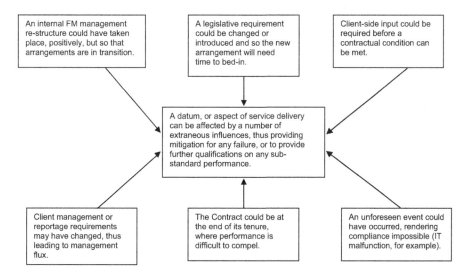

Figure 5.8   **Examples of mitigating circumstances that will affect an audit opinion**

To illustrate how looking at a fact in the round could assist in seeing something tried to be hidden:

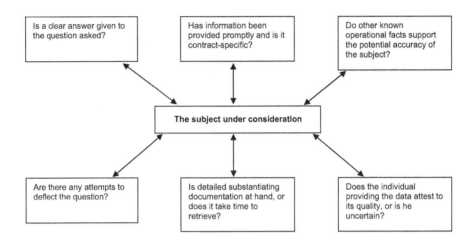

Figure 5.9 **An illustration of the kinds of questions that should illuminate if something is being hidden**

Seeing any subject in the round means to take the area under examination, and look at it for extenuating and contributing circumstances for its success or failure, or to assist in seeing if attempts are being made to hide the truth of performance. Auditors will regularly speak of this technique, and the others outlined, in the same breath, knowing that different nuances between the techniques will show up different aspects.

For example:

Once upon a time there was a contractor who absolutely didn't want any examination made of a standard of decoration. Approaching the client directly, the contractor attempted to show why any formal examination of 'reasonable decoration' was an impossibility (given the subjectivity of the adjective). This was a good move on the contractor's part — a month was gained before the client opined. The inspection was scheduled a few weeks hence, and the contractor showed up with a large number of colleagues — the auditors were never lonely in the (agreed) joint inspection.

The large group of colleagues meant that it was difficult for the audit team to concentrate. As soon as one element of substandard decoration was noticed, a long joint debate would immediately ensue as to whether the target of 'reasonable' had indeed been met in the room, in the corridor, within the context of the building itself. The auditors, in this particular instance, had no choice but to leave the field of battle, and resume again another day.

What the auditors discovered in the days subsequent to the site visit, though, as the subject was not closed, was that what was trying to be concealed was the lack of any published corporate costed plan for dealing with redecoration (a rolling programme). The auditors opined that generally the standard of decoration was relatively poor, but that the major failing was to not be able to demonstrate that a corporate plan was in place to keep any 'non-reasonable decorative disorder' instances to a minimum.

Giving credit where credit is due — if the plan of swamping the audit team with distractions was deliberate — it worked reasonably well. Even better — if the contractor did know that the true non-compliance/performance was lack of forward planning (which carried a heavier financial penalty), and did use this strategy of distraction to delay the question being asked — the ploy was a fair attempt. The contractor effectively delayed the day of reckoning, and was probably content with this delay (if nothing else).

Seeing an 'issue in the round' then can sometimes mean, for an auditor, to look at how an issue is being presented, and to see if any undue emphasis is being placed anywhere in order to fascinate the auditor sufficiently to not enquire further about the true audit subject matter. It involves a degree of examination of the individual or corporate reaction to a legitimate audit question. If a contract plan is not to hand, how can any individual within the team be expected to operate within it? If a contract plan is to hand, but an individual is hesitant about providing it, what does that mean about the plan itself?

Auditors use the technique to understand the context and all contributory factors to any service provision. To illustrate further:

- In order to present a service failure fault where it properly belongs, a good performance auditor will attempt to see the failure in its proper corporate context. For example: Is the failure a result of lack of corporate support to the site team? Did any client-side indecision delay implementation sufficiently so that knock-on effects are still being felt? To what degree do those factors influence the result found? Were there actions that could have been taken to mitigate any overall failure? Was the failure critical, and so a means should have been found to overcome it regardless of any corporate context?

- If a service failure is found, how does that failure 'fit' within its larger subject area? If a PPM system is faulty, does that mean that the engineering service, in general, is suspect? Ultimately, is that one failure greater than its seeming weight within the contract?

- If no adequate training records are kept, does that mean a conceivable failure in training, or a failure in record keeping? The failure here could be a failure to ensure all personnel are demonstrably properly trained to undertake their duties — and specifically in an H&S context. The failure could also mean a simple administrative misstep, and where records were due to be updated within days of the audit.

Seeing any subject matter in the round means, finally, being able to step back from what is presented, to see it in its true context. If a contractor says 'this is where our true success lies in this area, and I really don't understand why you persist in asking the question you are', it is a fairly safe bet that the auditor's original question was a good one. If a contractor says 'I'm providing this for you, but I don't see its relevance', it is fairly automatic that the information is meaningless and pointless to site operation.

Auditors will always take care to note why something is being said, or not said, or why some data is chosen to be presented, in any audit situation.

The roundness of any particular audit subject is seeing all aspects that influence that area of concern — and these influences can also be client-led — in order to understand its true strength or weakness. It differs from all other audit techniques in that it steps back from the physical operation of the contract to see what might be an affect, or a contributory factor, in the widest possible context.

REASONABLENESS AND HOW TO SEE WHAT IS REASONABLE IN CONTEXT

The consideration of 'reasonableness' will be the most subjective aspect to any audit, and therefore the element most likely to be debated if any assessment is negative.

Reasonableness has one base in Health & Safety legislation, where the standard of undertaking an action 'within reason' needs to be critically assessed. Reasonableness will also be seen in elements of FM specifications describing a qualitative element of decoration, or cleanliness or other primarily soft services.

In Health & Safety terms, auditors do look very critically at the action meant to be undertaken, and will always err on the side of caution. That is to say that, any auditor will expect a greater effort to be made if at all possible, in order to encourage all parties to make buildings under their control to be as safe as possible. Reasonableness in Health & Safety legislation means, though, that it is expected that actions are taken in the context of proportionality to the potential event.

As an example here: if a lift is undergoing maintenance and the contractor finds he has only one traffic cone which stops individuals approaching the open lift, any auditor is likely to expect another member of the contractor team standing beside that cone to ensure it is seen. The auditor will take the view that an open lift shaft should be more protected — reasonably — than one unsecured traffic cone.

Another H&S example might be if a procedure for disseminating H&S information to site staff is not in place. Here, it cannot be demonstrated that site staff understand any risk assessments that should be undertaken before a task, or procedures to follow in the event of an incident/emergency. The auditor will take the view that a major failure has occurred, as FM site staff will themselves be at ongoing risk. Reasonably, here, all site staff must have an ongoing cognisance of H&S mandates throughout their work.

Standards of reasonable decorative order, or reasonable provision of soft services generally, are yet more complex. While H&S 'reasonableness' can be looked at as a series of practical actions and whether they do or do not assist in their main purpose — of protecting persons — soft service standards will always be largely subjective.

The standard of reasonableness is a mechanism that was incorporated into specifications some years ago, and was meant to reduce prescriptive descriptions of service provision. Prescriptive specifications would say things like 'millimetres of dust on a window sill acceptable, or not'; or 'grassed areas not being allowed to grow further than xx millimetres during the summer months'. 'Reasonableness' was adopted as an occasional standard to get around the need to measure any element precisely to confirm compliance/non-compliance, and was meant to recognise that the client/contractor would be happy to use their best collaborative efforts to agree the specific degree of acceptability on the ground, at the time. The standard of reasonableness was meant to ultimately save on public sector management time.

Reasonable standards of whatever kind can be easy to identify when they are very good or very bad. If a building's corridor has flaking paint, dented skirting boards and a missing internal blind, it would be very difficult for anyone to argue that they represent 'good decorative order'. If that same corridor, however, looks a bit dusty, a bit shabby, the missing blind is only one of 30, arguing whether or not these perceptions are reasonable is more difficult.

The point of this is context, at least partially. In order to understand if that corridor is, in fact, in unreasonable decorative order, one must see that corridor in the context of a series of elements:

- the prescribed rolling redecoration programme (whether the programme, overall, is being adhered to, or not);

- the corridor itself as compared to other corridors (are the standards noticeably the same, or different);

- the corridor within any discrete sub-elements (are some decorative standards those of cleaning, rather than decoration proper, for example);

- any further guidelines within the specification itself (do any overarching guidelines exist as to standards expected, or not. An example here might be within a hospital, where sterile standards might be expected, or a prestige headquarters building, where high standards are described 'as befitting a prestige corporate building).

If an auditor were to assess that corridor, he would use those contexts to understand — and so to be able to demonstrate — any assessment made. A clear demonstration of contractor laxity in undertaking reasonable decorative works would result in an opinion that more can be done to achieve the standard of reasonableness generally outlined. Even here, given the subjective nature of the term, any contractor will generally be able to argue that standards, while perhaps not optimum, do not result in a specific service failure. If that corridor can be used, if it is safe to use, the offices themselves are fairly clean, any contractor is likely to say that the overarching requirement is being met (and we'll clean up that corridor in due course).

An auditor here, listening to the contractor here, will take his point, but place it within the series of contexts described above. All data will be placed in the context of the success/failure of any sub-elements, and an assessment that is less subjective (but not completely so) will be arrived at.

The pragmatic way of agreeing any assessment of reasonableness/unreasonableness is through joint inspections between client and contractor. These joint inspections, which should be documented, are a useful tool to establish a working dialogue on mutual expectations. Optimally, having this strategy of joint-inspections on reasonable standards should be agreed at the time of Contract Let. Doing so provides a strong basis for an ongoing constructive dialogue about expectations from both parties.

In this joint inspection of this hypothetical corridor, both 'sides' are likely to take different views — for all obvious reasons. If both 'sides' have the ability to produce action, then, pragmatic agreements can be made on the spot, and without the need for any more long-winded discussions on the subject. The client can demand, and the contractor can explain. Somewhere in the discussion will be the solution that has the potential to work for all.

Using the mechanism for joint inspections of property for standards of reasonableness in soft services is most effective. Auditors can be used for assessment of reasonable standards of the performance of soft services, and especially if joint inspections have not taken place, or if relations between client/contractor are antagonistic. Similar techniques to joint inspections can be used here, or a more aggressive approach of photographic evidence used to underpin assessments made.

Specialists should always be used for any assessment of whether or not Health & Safety standards are being complied with. No lay person has the ability to assess such specialist requirements, and clients should always take care that specialists continue to be used regularly in any contract to assist in their discharging of their own duty of care.

KPIS, SFDS AND THEIR ASSESSMENT

Introduction

The Office of Government Commerce (OGC) defines Performance Indicators as: 'the means for measuring and assessing supplier performance using a robust and agreed set of criteria.' Key Performance Indicators (KPIs) are those Performance Indicators that are seen to be of most import to client-side management and the contract's performance — therefore 'Key'.

KPIs are routinely agreed, presented and discussed as a formal supplier confirmation of the adequacy of performance against negotiated targets.

The OGC goes on to say that Indicators need to be:

S	Specific
M	Measurable
A	Actionable
R	Realistic
T	Timely

To expand slightly on OGC's pithy outline of what KPIs should be, those constructing performance indicators should ensure that they are:

- Specific enough to describe precisely the area/service to be considered

- Measurable so that the indicators can be quantified

- Actionable so that the area being measured can be readily subject to change

- Realistic so that they don't expect unachievable actions

- Timely so that performance indicators can be measured in sufficient time so as to provide up-to-date management information.

OGC is clear that KPIs should provide an equitable approach to improve outcomes and enable risk identification and mitigation — in other words, that KPIs should provide a clear impetus for a contractor to improve performance, but not so that their fulfilment becomes unduly onerous (and therefore expensive).

In PFI Contracts, KPIs tend to be constructed through a mirror image. In PFI Contracts, a mechanism of Service Failure Defaults (SFDs) are used to show both the level of service expected, and with a clear financial penalty if those standards are not achieved during a specific period of time. While non-PFI Contract KPIs can be written fairly broadly, and often are, PFI SFDs tend to be constructed on a very prescriptive basis.

For example, and using hypothetical KPIs/SFDs here, the difference between the two might be:

	Non-PFI	**PFI**
Landscaping	Soft landscaping should be kept free of detritus and present an acceptable standard at all times	Grass must be cut to within 4 centimetres at all times between the months of June and September
Cleaning	The offices must be clean at the commencement of any working day	Cleaning must be undertaken to ensure no staining, marks or adhesions, dust or dirt, smearing and finished appropriately to the material being cleaned
Reactive maintenance	Reactive maintenance should take place so as to continue the good running of the building at all times	Reactive maintenance must take place within 10 minutes, 1 or 2 hours, or 1 day, of being reported to the Helpdesk

HM Treasury has put increased value on agreeing reasonable KPIs/SFDs at the time of Contract Let, recognising their inherent value to all concerned. In Version 4 PFI Contract Guidance HM Treasury recommends the establishment of a manual or user guide to support effective monitoring, and recommends that a 'dry run' of these arrangements takes place prior to financial close. This dry run is meant to test how the performance mechanism would work in practice, and what affect ongoing monitoring will have on departmental/authority staff.

Critically too, HM Treasury goes on to say:

> *'(The performance measurement system) … must be user friendly. An over-complex mechanism risks being ignored in practice. Where it is necessary to have a complex structure, consideration should be given to what in practice might be the distinction between features applied on a day-to-day basis and those which are designed to ward off specific potential problems … '.*

Whether Treasury guidance is reflected in performance mechanisms or not, all KPIs/SFDs are normally reported to client on a monthly basis, and should contain unequivocal statements of adherence to the standards identified. The idea of KPI reportage is a form of self-certification of performance by any contractor. They are meant to alleviate a client-side management burden of assessing performance on a regular basis, and should therefore provide any contractor's client with reasonable assurance that all is functioning as it should be on the contract.

Further, KPIs/SFDs should clearly indicate where and when a fault occurred, so that proactive management actions can be taken — this is a clear potential value of KPIs. Given the complexity of all FM contracts, having any advance warning of existing/potential problems gives both client and contractor teams sufficient time to understand why the failures might be existing, and what steps should be taken to improve.

Typical KPIs work numerologically, and that is to say that KPIs are constructed so that actions should be either limited in time (an action completed within a certain time-period) or cumulatively (where numbers of actions undertaken/incomplete are added up). With both, there will be a level of pass/fail where if the KPI calculation doesn't meet the base standard expected the service is seen to be failing. While this is true, our experience of KPI assessment has shown that it is easy for KPI calculations to become so complex that the truth of the data is almost impossible to verify.

Generally too, KPIs and SFDs tend to be fairly resistant to change. If a great deal of management effort has been expended on their construction and management implementation, it becomes difficult to consider altering them in any way — even to suit changed business priorities. Changing KPIs/ SFDs mid-contract means that assessment of performance over the contract's lifespan becomes more difficult, as different performance parameters need to be compared. This ultimately leaves the possibility open that KPIs/SFDs do become a fairly meaningless management exercise, done for forms sake, and without serving any long-term purpose.

As a basic, KPIs/SFDs should provide the following rudimentary performance information:

- if contractor H&S obligations are being discharged properly

- if financial targets and obligations are being met

- if maintenance is on track, and so that any need for greater reactive maintenance/plant replacement might be reduced

- trend analysis of uptake of individually costed services (for example, catering)

- trend analysis of customer satisfaction across services.

Whatever the difficulties might be with these systems, KPIs/SFDs can help the client management team to be forewarned, so they can be forearmed. This is only true if KPI/SFD assessment is realistic and can be seen to be unequivocally true.

Assessment of KPIs and SFDs

Assessing FM KPIs or PFI Contract SFDs are identical in their intent, and demand identical audit forms. The assessment of either is where an auditor is asked to confirm that the KPI adherence/lack of SFDs attributable is as the contractor has said. For ease, we will use the term KPIs for the rest of this section as a shorthand to denote both KPIs and SFDs, unless the difference is material between them.

Given then that assessment of KPIs or SFDs is looking back in time, assessment of both is largely a paper-based exercise. Techniques identified throughout this chapter would be used, singly and in combination.

The basic question asked by an auditor to the contractor would always be: 'How do you know this statement is true?' The contractor would be expected to show his management process for the KPI computation, and an auditor would then attempt to duplicate the result. If the duplication was positive, the auditor would then look for ways the KPI could be subverted in any way. The auditor would look to see if other contributory data that would affect the computation should legitimately be included in the assessment, or not. The decisions on which data might be legitimately included, and how to find it, would be influenced by the other techniques contained throughout this book.

Problems arise threefold, aside from the normal audit processes, however, in determining the veracity of information collated and presented:

- KPIs tend to be constructed using complex mathematical equations, where the computation of what is compliant/non-compliant in terms of achieving a peformance level is opaque in the extreme.

- KPIs tend to ask questions that are difficult and time-consuming to quantify in themselves. A KPI saying that all Helpdesk calls need to be answered within five rings, for example, could only be proved by manually assessing each call made from original IT records. As a client, therefore, one can only trust the data given or commit oneself to a time-consuming exercise to attempt to discover if KPIs as presented were accurate.

- SFDs tend to be based on micro-detail of contract performance. Given the complex management processes needed to support this micro-detail, it is difficult to prove compliance/non-compliance because of the myriad of mitigating circumstances that might qualify any result.

These issues are discussed below.

For example:

If the subject is the fulfilment of reactive maintenance tasks within a month, the statement of compliance here (adherence to a KPI) might be expressed as:

- the number of reactive tasks undertaken against PPM tasks

- with days subtracted for weekends and holidays

- reactive works that were client requests

- and the percentage within those left that were delivered within specified periods of time (and these would be variable).

For an auditor to understand the truth of any statement made, a line-by-line read of a Helpdesk system (which produces the records on which the analysis is made) would need to be undertaken, calendar in hand, and with a step-by-step analysis of whether the statement was true on a cumulative basis using many of the techniques identified elsewhere and the contractor's own computational roadmap.

The diagram below outlines the broad steps needed to be taken overall in assessing KPI accuracy regarding reactive maintenance (as an example):

To illustrate, this example:

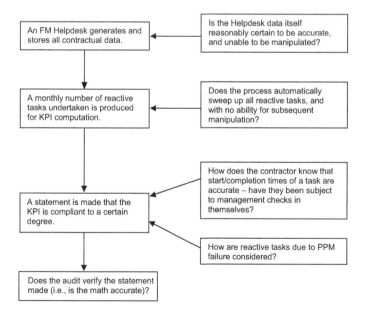

Figure 5.10   An example of how to ascertain KPI compliance, with reactive maintenance as an example

To illustrate, more generally for SFDs (all of which would have to be confirmed as true or false):

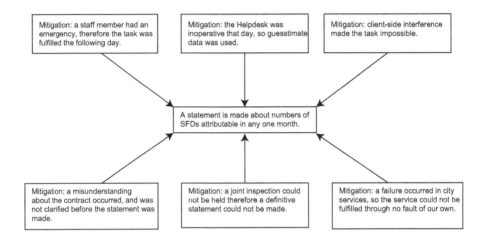

Figure 5.11   An example of how to assess SFD accuracy

Understanding KPI/SFD compliance therefore is an audit task like any other. Determining the truth of an issue involves understanding it using the various techniques contained throughout this book.

The complication of KPI/SFD auditing is through the often impenetrability of the contractor assessment formulae used, and the micro-detail that is sometimes supplied.

However, by breaking down any one element into its component part, any auditor can assess if a true statement is being made, or not, given time. Given that the auditor will be attempting to trace a contractor's unequivocal statement, and then looking at how that process could be misrepresented, auditing a KPI/SFD is only a discrete aspect of any audit protocol.

Conclusion

KPI/SFD assessment is an audit subject like any other, with the exception that an auditor is automatically looking back in time, and attempting to prove/disprove a statement made by a contractor as to compliance and the contractor's self-certification of his performance.

Confirmation of KPI/SFD accuracy of reportage is made more complex, however, by the relative opacity of data construction, or the large numbers of extenuating circumstances that can be brought to bear. Assessment of accuracy in this area, therefore, differs from other audit subjects in the time that needs to be spent by any auditor in determining the veracity of data presented.

Many clients have issues with KPI construction, where they do not provide sufficient detail or are so impenetrable as to be meaningless. HM Treasury and the Office of Government Commerce both recommend that KPIs/SFDs are negotiated as part of any Contract Let, so that they can provide meaningful client data, without disproportionate client time.

Incidentally, we have developed a KPI system that answers most of the problems presented in this brief section. This KPI system is more transparent and so is easier to understand and to prove. It is fully flexible, where different elements can be brought in or out, without any disproportionate contractor/ client involvement in doing so. It can attach financial penalties at any point, or not.

Summary

Audit techniques are interrelated, and some have close connections to each other. Each are different though, and assist an auditor in breaking down his subject into individual components that are capable of being assessed in their own right, and within the overarching contract and other policy and business requirements as a whole.

To summarise the above chapter, then:

'Seeing clearly' is simply the means by which an auditor will break down an audit subject into components capable of being analysed. This isolation of auditable components can be complex — as in Health & Safety legislation — or more simply — the standard of reasonable cleaning. Seeing clearly allows an auditor to delineate elements that are compliant and non-compliant, and for further analysis.

An auditor's independence from any influences brought to bear is fundamental to a successful audit. Any vested interests by any party should be considered as such, and effectively to have no bearing on the audit's findings.

Simply, any anecdotal information or expression of 'suspicion that all is not well' should be treated as interesting, but to have no effect on the audit itself unless verified elsewhere.

Transparency of data is one of the concepts most often misunderstood by any audit subject. Site performance and management systems are intrinsically interlinked. Each supports the other, and each must be able to be seen clearly as interrelated concepts to be fully transparent. Transparency of data is fundamental to the public sector, as it allows the greatest possible certainty that the contract is running as expected, and without the ability for its misuse.

The ability to look at any issue on both a micro and macro level, vertically/horizontally, and in the round, is fundamental. While any auditor should be able to see any issue in its proper context, it ultimately falls to the audit team leader to see the audit in overview, and so that robust assessments can be made of any issues weight within the audit as a whole.

An audit that only looks at systems, or at site performance, is likely to misunderstand a true performance level. If systems are transparent, and all appears to be in order in process descriptions, one would expect to see a verified and clear reflection of that performance level on site. If, on the other hand, building users are generally content about performance standards, but the contract is operating in a management void (to some degree or another), the contract is still failing because the contractor cannot demonstrate his overall compliance in management terms.

Seeing in the round involves understanding of any other legitimate affects on the running of the contract. Clearly, criticising a contractor for any inaction when that lack of action is due to circumstances outside of his control would be unfair. There may be instances where a temporary hiatus in compliance is justified and understandable, or some degree of mitigation exists for any failure found. Seeing in the round allows an auditor to further contextualise his findings, so that an overly negative assessment can be mitigated.

Standards of reasonableness, including reasonableness in Health & Safety legislation, is the most difficult subject for an auditor to assess properly. If 'reasonable' can be defined as 'acceptable and according to common sense', the subjective element will always remain. Seeing what is reasonable in context, therefore, involves subjecting any subject to a variety of tests to see what is equitable to both sides of any contract. Finally here, our opinion is that the best way of resolving any questions as to reasonable standards (save for H&S) is through joint client/contractor inspections, where issues needed to be resolved can be done so on the spot, and with all immediacy.

KPI and SFD assessment is an audit subject like any other, and testing KPI or SFD data can be undertaken like any other subject. Given the complexity of most KPI/SFD constructions, and the significant amount of mitigating circumstances that are likely to be posited, a robust analysis of accuracy in self-certification by any contractor is likely to be a time-consuming exercise. If any client throughly relies on KPI/SFD data to confirm contractual compliance overall:

- regular tests should be made of that data to confirm its robustness, or;

- KPI/SFD constructs should be written so as to be as unambiguous, meaningful and verifiable as possible.

6

Management Issues for Auditors

Introduction

The preceding chapters have discussed how to audit, and have described various structures and audit techniques. This chapter goes back to another basic, and is meant as an aide-memoire for auditors themselves.

Executing an audit also means preparing and agreeing a robust audit brief, commissioning the right team of auditors and drafting a report that will withstand all objections. These are management issues for any audit team leader, and have a strong effect on the audit itself.

Choosing an audit team in a contentious audit will be a different choice than for a modular audit. Writing a report with the knowledge of potential litigation is likely to be quite different from an audit constructed in any partnering sense.

There are connections though, of clarity, of clear demonstrations of fact, and of a considered view of what strategy and team are best likely to deliver the result demanded of the audit itself.

Audit Preparation

PREPARING THE AUDIT BRIEF

An audit brief does not need to be a detailed chapter and verse discussion of what is to take place, but rather a perfectly summarised view of the issues under consideration, confirmation of dates and audit team, commitment to reporting and the protocol for doing so and note made of client involvement sought. While any audit brief is generally confidential between the client/auditor – to state the obvious, again – it should be written so as to be seen by anyone, and that any very sensitive information is treated separately.

An audit brief, therefore, should specify:

a)   The Instruction: What audit is being commissioned

b)   Dates of audit: Start/end

c)   The Audit Team: With attached CVs and including any specialism that they are specifically to examine

d)   Reporting: Draft report, debriefing meetings and final reports, and their timings

e)   Client-side involvement: Where input might be needed

f)   Limitations to the brief: Where the audit brief might be derailed, by whom and how and its effect

g)   Cost.

Keeping an audit brief relatively concise – say, two pages – is in recognition that the majority of detailed discussions/decisions will have been made face-to-face. Producing a succinct professional outline of the task commissioned provides a cornerstone for the auditor/client to know if the audit was successful or not, at any subsequent debrief on the process as a whole.

CHOOSING AND INSTRUCTING THE AUDIT TEAM

Audit teams should be chosen for specialist expertise – this is obvious. Less obvious, perhaps, is that personal characteristics of different audit team members can also be brought into play during the site audit itself. By that we mean auditors can be requested to downplay or to bring to the fore elements of their personality which can influence what data is found or evidence given in any formal interview. While thinking like this might sound a touch manipulative, which it is, none of it is dirty pool, and is a perfectly legitimate factor to consider.

We will return to auditor manipulation in a minute, but it's worth mentioning that performance auditing is a specialist professional endeavour, and there are not huge numbers of individuals out in the world who declare themselves to be solely auditors or to have that specialist expertise. Our feeling, though, is that there are genuine experts working away happily in their chosen profession, who have the nature of an auditor in themselves – a sense of enquiry, an interest in seeing the rights or wrongs of an issue, a sense of independence. Choosing an auditor, therefore, can mean finding an expert who hasn't undertaken an audit before, and using him carefully and well.

Instructing an auditor can be done diversely too. While sharing the basics of the audit (type of contract, scope of audit, timescales and so on) is a given, the audit leader can take a view on the following:

- showing the Contract/Specification to the team or not

- forbidding any verbal communication with those being audited beyond pleasantries

- requesting the opposite – to be as communicative as possible, to try to gather as many 'on site perceptions' as possible (NB, these perceptions cannot be used in an audit, but can influence where an auditor looks)

- relating any client background to the audit, or not.

And to discuss briefly:

SHOWING THE CONTRACT, OR NOT

The choice of showing the Contract/Specification or not to the audit team is not as ill-considered as it may appear. One should remember, of course, and aside from anything else, that any auditor going to look at any building contract will have a good working knowledge of the types of Contracts/Specifications extant in the industry at large. Any auditor going to audit without seeing the precise Contract/Specification concerned is not going in as blind as it might first appear.

The occasions on which one would send in an auditor that cold are few and far between. However, there are occasions on which it is of value to the audit overall for an auditor to simply see the issues before him, without recourse to the Specification/Contract.

These instances might include when the audit is systems based, (and so the auditor will only look at how management systems mesh according to best practice), or when the specification itself it hugely elaborate (most PFI Contracts …) and to such an extent that the time taken to master its contents would be disproportionate to the scope of the audit. These two examples are important. Not showing a complex PFI contract to an auditor won't make affect him negatively, but will save a reasonable expenditure of time and money on that auditor becoming fully conversant with its detail. If a single auditor's brief is to look at a simple area of performance/compliance, that auditor has no need to understand the contract overall, but simply its overall parameters. Similarly, if an audit is systems based, there will be few specific contractual obligations that will affect his examination. While looking at the contract might be generally interesting to the auditor, its contents won't affect how the audit might be carried out.

In the circumstances where the choice is made **not to** show the Specification/ Contract to one's audit team, the audit team leader has the primary responsibility of ensuring that the audit protocol and findings conform to the Specification/ Contractual expectations. To state the obvious (again), at regular points, the audit team leader should discuss individual progress in detail on an ongoing basis, and so to correct any misapprehensions about the detail of the Contract/ Specification.

There is one final advantage in one's audit team of this approach – that of maximum clarity. The audit team leader, by the time an audit starts, is likely to be immersed in the subject, and will be fully aware of all nuances in play during its conduct. Given that, having an audit team which has no knowledge of, and has been instructed to care less, about the contract detail, means that they have a better chance of seeing clearly only that which is clearly presented to them.

In a way, and the strategy is really only undertaken in exceptional circumstances, the auditors will be able to debate what is found in the context of best practice and public sector policy, and to have the specific contractual problems brought in afterwards. In a way, again, this strategy potentially allows for maximum clarity by bringing in an extra audit dimension for the client's future use (in placing the audit findings within industry standards at large, and so to assist in any mid-term planning).

Forbidding any communication

The tactic of forbidding any communication by the audit team with those being audited can be undertaken for two reasons: because the audit itself is deeply contentious and may slip into litigation; or because the audit team leader wishes to present as intimidating an appearance as possible, and to ensure that the auditors are not distracted by any extraneous information whatsoever.

Undertaking an audit with the possibility of litigation is a slightly piquant experience. Undertaking an audit with the clear knowledge that lawyers are not far away is a guarantee that auditors are not welcomed with open arms, and a guarantee that every move made, every request for information, and every casual word spoken will be reported to senior contractor corporate management and analysed. In these circumstances, it does behove the audit team leader well to control communication carefully, so that there are witnesses to any conversation about the contract/audit, and so that no uncontrolled dialogue about any issue takes place.

Choosing relative silence as an intimidatory tactic is, again, fairly rare, and can be chosen when the audit team leader is well aware that the contract being audited is felt by the private sector to be a pushover. This is to say that the tactic can be used as a fair piece of audit theatre, to demonstrate to the FM Contractor that the audit is perhaps more serious than they thought, and to command full respect for its progress.

Both reasons above, and there are doubtless others, provide the added value of giving the audit team peace and quiet, and the ability to concentrate fully on their assigned subjects. While audits do tend to be conducted in a kind of purdah, they can also be fairly interruptive – after all, no one can possibly protest at endless piecemeal provision of information, can they?

The friendly approach

Asking auditors to go on a charm offensive is another clear tactic, and with its own clear value. Given that it matters little what people say to you during an audit – save for formal recorded interviews – any charm offensive can only result in the provision of subsidiary information to be confirmed by other means. Overheard conversations or finding that special person with an axe to grind against their own firm can provide valuable insights into another fruitful area of discovery.

This is another manipulative tactic of course. The friendly approach does try to capitalise on occasional individual's desire to please, by asking the most awkward of questions in the most sympathetic manner possible.

In a truly hypothetical example here, we generally know that engineers often feel undervalued and a conversation with an engineer can easily turn to the problems in dealing with management who, they believe, don't understand the problems of a PPM system in a changing environment. This in turn can lead to a few opinions that might be worth checking on the PPM system itself, or about a potential management laxity that could affect the contract's good running.

Drafting and Presentation

A WHOLE DIFFERENT LANGUAGE

Our work as auditors has consistently shown that the private sector finds it difficult to read and understand public sector corporate imperatives, and that this difficulty may be based in the particular language used by their clients and auditors.

Public sector language has developed over the years to contain precise meanings within a wealth of policy background. The use of any qualifying words, or the choice not to qualify a statement, can make a huge difference.

For example:

- 'We request direct action on the subject.'

- 'We request a discrete examination of the subject.'

- 'We request action in due course on the subject.'

means in turn:

- Take unambiguous action now.

- Look privately at the subject for verbal report back.

- We're not that fussed, but are writing it as a marker to protect ourselves if the subject ever appears again.

In auditing terms, the use of qualifying words or grammatical stress words will express clearly to all levels of contentment/disquiet. For example: 'For clarity, our opinion is that a comprehensive failure occurred', means that the auditor is taking care that all who read the report cannot ignore the opinion. On the other hand: 'We take note of a seeming non-compliance' relays a qualified opinion as to a potential failing that does not need to be acted upon immediately.

An audit report can be fairly shocking to read for those being audited – this is really understandable, and auditors will be deliberate in causing that shock, or not, through their choice of language. At various times, we have found ourselves amazed at reactions to what we considered to be a relatively positive and innocuous report. Granted, if the opening line of an executive summary says 'We found significant areas of non-compliance throughout the subjects studied and wish to state clearly that the performance of the contract appears to be fundamentally lacking in any management', it might be best for the contract manager to go swiftly into a dark quiet room for a time.

If, however, that opening line says 'Our audit showed that, while some areas of our audit subject throw up issues of concern, the contract appears to be broadly functioning appropriately', one can rest assured that nothing too nasty lurks within the body of the report.

The point here is context and balance. The civil service, like auditors, works with precise language. This language is intended to embrace nuance, so that readers can be completely clear about elements that might influence opinions, or which call for different kinds of specific, or more general, action.

Similarly, any body being audited should remember that any report or action is taken with the clear knowledge of how that report/action fits within public sector policies of the day. As governments come and go, nuances of political philosophy impact directly on the civil service and how they might approach any subject under their aegis. Trickling down to any mandate for performance auditing, changes in public sector policy might mean that VFM auditing is less important than, say, ensuring that any contract is seen to work.

Therefore, any property contractor/FM manager should be able to readily understand public sector policy imperatives that are likely to influence civil service management strategies by simply regularly looking at HM Treasury, Office of Government Commerce or National Audit Office websites. Having this knowledge will allow any FM Contractor – in broad terms – to understand the constraints that their clients are operating within, and how they might expect that management to impact on them over the short-mid-term. This in turn will allow the contractor to understand why a particular type of audit regime might be foisted upon them, or why their public sector managers might concentrate on one issue over another, over any short or long period of time.

The Audit Report

SUMMARISING THE AUDIT – PRE-REPORT

A good audit team will share their information throughout the progress of any audit – between the team itself, and with the client if he wishes. End-of-day conversations about general findings tends to be useful, so that the team can compare notes, and where any management issues that might occur across service streams can be teased out. The audit team leader will use these conversations to provide valuable information about whether or not any auditor should concentrate more on one area than another, or to change the overall emphasis perhaps through a time-limited focus on one particular overarching area. Through these conversations, as well as at the conclusion of the audit, a good audit team leader will ask his auditors for their best opinion as to relative success or failure, and will track that opinion to see how it changes. This forming of initial opinions assists in finally assessing success/failure in overall terms, as it provides maximum professional input into the audit subject's overall performance.

Another knack, therefore, of seeing the audit in terms of both micro and macro viewpoints is in its summation, and this would be done subject by subject, as well as through the findings of the audit as a whole. The ways and means by which such assessments are made are hugely diverse and will vary widely over time. The summation of success/failure in an audit – the executive summary – however, does provide an overall view on the relative health of any issue under consideration, and is a critical part of a good audit.

As examples:

- If any service stream shows consistent management issues or failures, and these issues have the potential to continue to multiply, or feed misleading information to the client, or to put the client or building occupants at any kind of risk, the auditor is likely to sharply criticise the contractor and recommend immediate detailed management action through a robust change management programme.

- If any one of these failures is critical – a major H&S non-compliance, for example, or through misrepresenting performance data – the auditor is likely to use stronger language, where the breach is spelled out in unequivocal language and so that the contractor can have no reason for not understanding his failure. Dependent on the contract, of course, the auditor will always recommend financial recompense in a failure that is critical to H&S compliance, or that can result in damage to any asset.

- If management failures/site practices are noticeable, and violate good industry practice and other industry norms, but have no real affect on the client's ability to discharge its own responsibilities, the auditor is likely to recommend that the contractor puts its house in order, and to clear up the discrepancies, as a matter of good business practice.

- If any individual failure can be seen as such (that is, as really an isolated event/failure/series of failures within the whole), the auditor will likely ring-fence the comment on the failure to be fully specific. Here, any report is likely to make an overall comment on the relative success/failure of the contractor on the audit as a whole, and make a particular comment on the one significant failure, noting that it should be considered almost as a separate issue.

DRAFTING THE REPORT

Audit reportage is, of necessity, dry. The auditor will assume that any readership is fully aware of the audit subject(s), and won't spend much time outlining why any subject was under consideration, or the relative importance of one aspect of a subject over another. Most audit reports – save the executive summary – will simply describe what was seen as clearly as possible, step-by-step, and so that the conclusions drawn from it will be self-evident.

How an auditor chooses to draft is too diverse to reasonably comment upon, although every auditor will do so with his copied evidence and other documentation by his side. Instructions to any audit team member will similarly differ, where an audit team leader might wish to have greater or lesser input at different stages of the process. Every audit is likely to go through several drafts as opinions are fine-tuned, and full clarity is achieved.

Much has been written in the wide range of business management books available as guidance for executive summaries – there is no need to comment further here. We might simply note that the executive summary in audit reports is as important as in any other public document. Given that the report itself will contain detailed technical analysis, and where only those most directly concerned with the subject will read and digest it fully, it is vital that the executive summary clearly summarises overall findings, and points the report's readership at particular areas that are vital to read. The executive summary is the highest-level view of the audit results, and the failures and successes found throughout the process should be clearly prioritised and weighted so that the public sector client team is able to act soundly and immediately.

It is axiomatic that a skill in drafting is in knowing what it is possible to leave out, and what is important to leave in. Different data 'titbits' might be of great interest to the auditor – sad but true – but will distract more than help in the final report. If part of an audit report is to tell a story, the narrative line should be as clear as possible, so that the document reads well and that the description of the subject feeds naturally into conclusions drawn.

The key here is to simply write what one saw, or the results of interviews, or to describe other verifiable data, as clearly as possible. This simple method allows the audit to be corrected on fact, if necessary, and allows the report's readership to see clearly why conclusions were drawn.

To go right back to basics, the auditor should:

- state clearly the record or subject under examination

- describe clearly its contractual context

- describe the individual tests the record/subject was subject to

- place those results in their relevant contexts

- state the opinion formed, and why, given the steps above.

The type of audit undertaken, the subject matter, client brief, and the results found will also impact on whether or not, or how, the audit team might choose to make its recommendations. If errors found are widespread and diverse, the audit team might recommend and draft a change management plan, where the parallel recommendation is to see the plan carried out step-by-step. If the audit is relatively straightforward, however, the audit team might simply wrap up its recommendations into a few lines of prose.

In terms of drafting recommendations, complexity generally demands a clear list of actions to be taken. If results are more clear-cut, and the audit itself is relatively uncontentious, it is a fair waste of time to put more effort into teasing out recommendations as they will be contained in the report's body.

PRESENTATION

An audit norm is to present the audit report firstly in 'draft' to the client, and for distribution to the contractor if so desired. The point of producing a draft report is to allow for correction of any factual mistakes, and to seek any client input that might be felt necessary.

We have undertaken audits where draft reports were issued to the contractor virtually simultaneously with the client management team, and (the majority) where the contractor was only given the final audit report.

In general, save in those circumstances where litigation might be being considered, it is far more constructive to the client/contractor working relationship if reports are issued in draft, and for open discussion between the three parties (auditor, client, contractor). In order to make the audit of most use to all, giving the contractor a clear opportunity to correct any factual errors, or to challenge any conclusions made, makes the audit results that much stronger. By having the opportunity, regardless of the outcome, the contractor will have bought into the audit results – either by seeing them clearly through discussion, or by accepting that the report is factually correct (and therefore not open to further argument).

If any report is presented in draft, the audit team will be content to be corrected on matters of fact and if any fact is successfully challenged to reconsider any conclusions drawn. Any audit report will only normally be corrected if the data allowing for a correction is something that could naturally have been seen at the time of the audit, but was not shown for understood reasons. In other words, the audit report is not likely to be corrected if the contractor says 'we chose not to show you then, but show you now', or if the contractor says that 'we know this is wrong, but our systems do not allow us to show you why'. The auditor will look at any data that is meant to show why a description or an opinion is wrong, only within the same terms of the audit itself – data must be clear and verifiable – and can be seen to have been present during the time-frame of the audit itself.

The opposite – where an audit report is presented to a contractor as 'final' – has its uses too. The audit contents might be significantly important or sensitive, so that the client might choose that the contractor only sees the report cold, and with no real opportunity to discuss the overall findings. Presenting an audit as final in such cases shows that the client has fully accepted the audit results, and is not prepared to enter into any significant conversations as to its findings. It shows corporate strength, in other words, and sends a clear message to the contractor that the report must be taken seriously.

Any auditor, by this time, is immersed in his subject and will be fully prepared to discuss any detail of the report (draft or final). Of course, audits can be presented by the entire team, or parts of it, or simply by the audit team leader. The audit team leader will make these recommendations to his client in advance (as regards the number of auditors present most beneficial to the discussion), and the choice of a small or larger team is likely to be based on the complexity of the subject/audit findings, or through need of any particular technical specialisms. Auditors will be prepared to explain any part of the report, in any detail applicable to the audit process itself, and will have been instructed by the audit team leader to be prepared to talk their audience through any part of it.

And finally, when an audit report has been accepted by the client or the client/contractor team, the audit 'stands' and serves as a milestone document showing an independent view of the subject concerned. An auditor's role ends at that point, unless requested to oversee any change management plan.

Summary

The choice of auditor, given the range of instructions that might be given to them, is not as straightforward as choosing a team with the right skill-set, though choosing audit teams with the right skill-sets is fully obvious, again. Auditors don't need to be chosen solely for their experience of audit, though an expertise is the area under consideration remains a given:

- The auditor doesn't necessarily need to have audit experience, if he is briefed carefully and his workings overseen in detail. There are times when the personal characteristics or professional specialisms, in themselves, make an individual a useful auditor for some audit scenarios.

- The auditor can be chosen also for personal characteristics – a naturally outgoing personality, the ability to make friends quickly or an intrinsic discretion. These personal characteristics are an element to consider when choosing an audit team, as long as the audit team leader is fully aware of why an individual has been chosen, and his relative position and weighting within the team as a whole.

Drafting must be undertaken so that the executive summary contains the careful assessment made of relative successes/failures, and so that immediate action can be taken if necessary on any one element.

Drafting of the report itself must show clearly the evidence examined and the assessment made so that the conclusions drawn from that evidence can be self-evident.

Our general recommendation, save for those situations that may involve litigation, is to present an audit report in draft form for a contractor's agreement prior to formal publication. Giving a contractor the ability to challenge any points of fact is a positive management move. Having contractor buy-in at an early stage assists in any change-management programme.

Finally, any audit team leader should take the same care in choosing an audit team, as he did in recommending the overall audit structure. Choosing an audit team unifies all the processes contained in this book, as they will reflect in their specialisms and personal characteristics, the techniques and strategies outlined elsewhere.

Appendix 1:
Long-term Monitoring and Management of FM Contracts: Working with a Government Department over Years

Introduction

We have been working with a central government department regularly over some 10 years, amongst a wide range of our other work across the public sector. The Department – now known as Communities and Local Government or 'CLG' – has been, over that time, and in sequence:

- Department of Transport/Department of Environment (DoE/DoT)

- Department of Environment Transport and the Regions (DETR)

- Department of Transport, Local Government and the Regions (DTLR)

- The Office of the Deputy Prime Minister (ODPM)

- The Office of the Deputy Prime Minister/Department for Transport (ODPM/DfT)

- Before assuming its latest incarnation (CLG).

For ease, the shorthand of CLG will be used here, unless a particular incarnation is significant. This brief appendix is to describe how the Department and their FM functions changed over the years, our role within it as their primary consultant auditors, and lessons that CLG has learned throughout that process. This description might be of some use to other government departments to compare their own experience with, or to assist in, their own ongoing work.

Client side building/FM managers have changed equally or more so than the Departmental name, and with each managerial change there have been concomitant changes in priorities, strategies and viewpoints on the range of subjects associated with managing prestige central London public sector properties. With few exceptions, one constant throughout these ongoing and significant changes has been the role of FM performance/contract auditing.

This chapter is meant to provide a case study of one Department's experience in auditing terms over this decade. CLG, throughout the regular and seismic changes that are natural in the public sector, has kept a consistent view that their contractors should be habitually tested, and the results used to encourage improvement in management and contract performance. While CLG has kindly given permission to talk about their audit work over the years, you will find this chapter deliberately opaque regarding specific audits.

CLG's History of FM Auditing

There was unlikely to have been a deliberate strategy within CLG to undertake a long-term audit/assessment strategy. However, what began as the use of outside consultants to advise on overall contractual and building occupancy issues, did become such a strategy, as the body of audit work began to show some practical dividends to the regularly changing management team.

In its earliest incarnation, CLG was just starting the process of outsourcing its FM arrangements. One contractor, effectively working as a Managing Agent for one building and supervising specialist service contracts held by the public sector, migrated to a role managing all three primary central London buildings. Consultants were used to opine on such issues as cost – to show that the new arrangement continued to represent VFM – and whether the new FM management could deliver the required service levels.

A parallel issue, of ongoing concern at the time, was that the soon-to-be ex-public sector building managers, who felt, naturally enough, that they were unnecessarily replaced in a job they were doing very well. At that time, public sector policy mandates began the shift to using the private sector to deliver services that were previously managed by the civil service. As consultants we worked with our clients to see that the new arrangements did bed in well, and to provide a variety of management advice, including audit.

At the same time as overseeing the new arrangements, we were requested to examine FM performance on a fairly regular basis, as the new arrangements continued to become established, and to provide what assurance or comment we could on areas of concern to the Department. Issues found – and many of them were based on the fact that the Managing Agent function had no direct contractual link to the now-sub-contractors providing specialist services – directly influenced the next procurement exercise, and the management of the contract over the 4–5 years it ran in that new form.

While changing public-sector property managers took different views on the relative importance of one technical issue over another, the audits themselves were generally seen to be useful to measure progress, or to provide the public sector with firm knowledge as to how the contracts were working during any managerial tenure. The audits did vary significantly and continually – in terms of their concentration on particular subjects, because of specific individual management styles, and the audit questions posed overall. Different management structures and strategies required different data to support or deny those plans. Individuals with different management preferences or areas of expertise looked for more robust analysis of one subject over another.

Regardless of these variances, the diverse audits were able to paint a picture of the progress of the contract over its lifespan – showing consistent areas of weakness or strength, of lax or robust management, of failure and success.

The audits were used directly to assist – though certainly not drive – the conduct of the subsequent CLG FM procurement exercise. The audits showed the limitations of previous arrangements, and therefore how the next contractor should **not** do things, or how management arrangements should **not** be structured. The audits helped remind the procurement management team of problems they had experienced and provided a kind of touchstone for some aspects of how the new arrangements would be structured to avoid those problems in the future.

The new contract was duly let, the new arrangements began to bed in, and the Department benefited from a time of consistent management. The audit regime continued – with a look at one aspect or another service/management area approximately every six months – relatively unabated for another two to three years. This period of management stability allowed for a fairly consistent audit story to be told, where the terms of any audit followed in a fairly straight line, building on the results of any previous audit, and where changing data was easy to follow over time.

CLG performance audits continue to date. With changes in the public sector management team again, their focus has shifted, but the new management regime is committed to following on from the audits first commissioned, with slightly broader terms, and on a regular basis.

CLG has shown the benefit of a long-term audit strategy – even though the strategy has not been particularly seamless. Any public sector manager, at any time, can point to a body of work demonstrating audit results, and steps taken to improve performance and use that data to inform current and future decisions. Any contractor involved can similarly point to the same audits as 'set in concrete' opinions as to issues that were seen to be closed out, or where performance was found to be satisfactory or excellent. Both sides can and do draw on historic audit reports to assist in current working. They provide a reasonable benchmark to show how far this particular estate performed over time.

Any public sector body considering a similar strategy can learn from CLG's experience – both in positive and negative senses. The consistency of commissioning of regular audits – even if the subject is diverse – does provide a great deal of management information that can continue to assist in current endeavours. In using one auditor over that time, the auditor's knowledge outside of reportage, contributes to the public sector corporate memory of this aspect of their business.

More negatively, changes in management and management priorities, did mean that data over time was not directly comparable. The use of one firm mitigated against these schisms, of course. The diversity of audit approaches undertaken did provide a wealth of data on every conceivable FM/building management subject.

In effect, with CLG, we became a part of the corporate memory of FM management over a long period of time. Our reports, and our individual memories, assisted new managers to understand why some decisions were taken as they were, and what the state of play was, in FM, for the management responsibilities they inherited. In the pure terms of consultants assisting a client, overall the CLG used our firm as consultants should properly be used – to support decision-making, to facilitate knowledge transfer, and to carry out work that should be seen to be independent and specialist.

The One-Firm Approach

There are advantages and disadvantages to commissioning one firm to undertake VFM/performance audits over a long period of time, as in the CLG strategy.

In general terms, advantages to a one-firm approach include:

- a strong and deep auditor understanding of the individual client corporate ethos, its management structures, and how that might change (and so change expectations/priorities);

- an auditor that is fully aware of the detail of the contract/specification concerned, so that ongoing learning curves are not undertaken with each exercise – this saves time and money;

- a contribution to the long-term management of the contract, through regular independent reportage as to its 'state of play' and specific compliance levels at regular intervals.

Contrarily, disadvantages might include:

- the auditor growing blasé about the process, or becoming too intimate with any one party to see any subject matter with sufficient clarity;

- the corollary of no regular fresh perspective, so that elements deserving praise or criticism are unable to be readily seen.

CLG now considers that the commissioning of an auditor over the period of a contract, and with a fairly broad remit (at time of commissioning) to assess contractual performance throughout its range of disciplines to have been a positive management move – and so is proactively doing so, rather than as a kind of management default. Commissioning one firm does provide for a consistency of approach, in overall terms, and so that the firm of auditors is able to continuously clearly advise as to the ramifications of previous work (so that it affects the future).

Finally, CLG found that by working with one firm over a long period of time contributed to their corporate memory and management of a contract that remained in flux itself. While CLG did and does use other consultants, of course, and their own Internal Audit department looks at elements of their FM contracts on a regular basis, CLG's use of one firm to consistently check performance of their building arrangements has proved valuable.

Regardless of any 'one firm' approach, the value of a long-term audit strategy is largely a value of consistency of reportage, the saving of management time through commissioning of an independent process to assist in FM/building evaluation, and by clear discharge of part of their public sector accountability requirements. This base advice is echoed throughout this book.

How the Client and Contractor Changes as a Result of the Process

Organisations change over time. Organisations also change, or can change, or should change, as a result of an audit or audit programme. While this book majors on the opportunities and pitfalls of auditing for the public sector, and so we concentrate on using audit to facilitate changes in their private sector contractors, audits can and should also influence client management of any contract under their purview. CLG's experience of audit over the years bears this out.

Simplest first:

CONTRACTOR CHANGE

Change tends to happen relatively organically – through internal management decisions, as part of a larger corporate strategy – or forced through circumstance. Audit, amongst other factors, can be a force for change through identifying contractual non-compliance that must be rectified. Ideally audits can contribute to an ongoing private sector organic change. By this, we mean an audit programme undertaken in a partnering sense can help precipitate management discussions about positive organic change rather than by strict audit criticisms.

CLG requested us at different times to use various techniques to influence change with its FM Contractor – from very formal to very informal off-the-record discussions. Both strategies had their uses to all, and were completely dependent on the particular circumstances of the time.

As you may have gathered, we have taken part of or witnessed very few audits where the process was not found to be hostile and confrontational by the contractor concerned, and this remained true of the CLG more often than not. Audits are generally felt to be – understandably but not true – a mechanism for the client to catch the contractor out, or a fairly meaningless exercise that only impinges on contractor management time.

With CLG, different incumbent FM Managers did take a more positive view, from time to time, when it was felt – on our part at least – that a more constructive dialogue could take place as to how performance could reasonably be improved. Where a watchful trust did develop, this audit process probably came closest to being able to assist any 'organic change', rather than through formal client-backed insistence.

This kind of dialogue is not possible the vast majority of time. The audit itself can be very contentious, or initial problems found to be so significant, or the client/contractor relationship so fraught, that anything other than silence and formal comment would be inappropriate and damaging. With CLG, and given our consistent work over the years, and during occasional times when the FM management regime itself was stable, this dialogue proved to be useful for all. 'Back door' communications could be given and received, informal and formal advice could be given relatively off-the-record, and questions asked/answered without resorting to formal communications of any kind.

CLG, at different times, with different client-side managers, requested we assist the FM Contractor in the run-up to any audit, or throughout the progress of their day-to-day work related to a previous or forthcoming audit. The times when this did happen were when the CLG client/contractor relationship was particularly strong, or when a particular manager wanted to use all best endeavours to have his contractor benefit from the audit process.

In a circumstance quoted elsewhere in this book, we were requested to work with the FM Contractor in the immediate run-up to an audit, so that there could be no question of the contractor **not** understanding what we were trying to understand, and why conclusions were what they were on the previous exercises. The contractor's reaction to previous audit reports, all relating to one area of management, had shown a real lack of comprehension as to why our concerns were being (increasingly vehemently) expressed, and CLG wished us to demonstrate why the failures were significant in the public sector's eyes. In effect, therefore, we were asked to preview the forthcoming audit in an informal scenario, where no records would be kept, and to show the contractor through specific real examples, where concerns had been found, and why we considered them as fundamental as we did.

Here, we effectively showed the contractor how we approached our understanding of the subject concerned, and showed them how we assessed the quality of their work and management. The client sat in on parts of the exercise, so it could clearly be seen to be a partnering exercise. While the exercise with the contractor was real enough, care was taken not to show all auditor 'tricks', but to give a clear description of 'why auditors look at a subject like we do' and, in effect, in this instance, what transparency means to the public sector.

This relatively extreme example of auditor/client/contractor cooperation did produce the benefits earnestly desired by all – the contractor duly had a 'eureka' moment, and our subsequent closed-door audit showed a step-change improvement. An aside here is that the informal audit described above was undertaken by only one member of our firm, and that member had no input into the subsequent 'real' audit. That way, there could be no question as to the objectivity of the proper exercise.

If we were to ask CLG today if they would recommend this exercise to others, they would probably say 'yes, dependent on the circumstances'. Given that audit work is meant to facilitate positive change – amongst other things – having an auditor carefully assist a contractor in understanding the purpose of the examination, and how the public sector does view a particular subject, is no bad thing. In this example, given our longevity as Departmental auditors, a harmonious discussion of problems found in order to positively affect progress, can only be seen as positive.

By far the norm, though, is where change for a contractor is a formal process, and follows the formal publication of any report. The area has been discussed elsewhere. In brief, then, influencing contractor change can generally be undertaken throughout the audit process, by your auditor, by the following means:

- by informal dialogue throughout the contract's progress, where a contractor is invited to discuss audit findings with the auditor directly at any point;

- by specific detailed guidance in a more formal setting, as to how to put a system/service right;

- by a formal change management programme, and where an auditor can confirm any subject closed off as it occurs;

- by a point-blank statement of requirement that is a closed subject until the next audit.

CLIENT CHANGE

Our experience is that audits tend to influence client change by exception, more than by requesting direct input into their parallel FM management affairs. This is to say that different audit results will show clear areas for concern, or not, and so that client involvement in their FM Contract over the following months may change in management nuance to reflect FM contractor managerial change.

If, for example, serious Health & Safety deficiencies were found, any client-side manager will be spending more time than usual being certain that those deficiencies were rectified properly so as to discharge his duty of care. If, however, all is well, the client manager can concentrate on the other thousands of issues flooding his desk without undue concern.

However, there are issues which would demand client-side change, and an audit of any FM contractor has the potential to see these, and to recommend that the client himself changes a management system or management input into the process.

Examples here might include:

- an internal agreement process being consistently delayed

- an internal agreement process being unnecessarily complex

- a lack of formal liaison regarding H&S and other statutory matters

- a lack of clarity regarding performance expectations.

Most auditors, if looking at any contractor subject, would also comment on any client impact on the subject if found to be relevant. In the interests of being fair, and also so as to provide the most rounded perspective and advice, most auditors will take the trouble to be clear as to any client input/lack of input affecting any problem found. There are occasional circumstances where, if problems are found to be pervasive, recommendations for client change are intrinsic to the proposed change management plan. Here the auditor's expectation is that the client will work at problem-solving and management change jointly with his contractor, and including internally on the public sector's own management regime if necessary.

Deciding to criticise one's client's management arrangements is not an everyday occurrence. In the case of CLG, on the whole, client side FM managers have been willing to accept constructive suggestions for alterations of arrangements in place. CLG has gone further at different times, and requested audit input into their own management structures as a discrete subject, and for comment to be made on whether staffing arrangements are sufficient for the tasks at hand, and can be seen to accomplish those tasks seamlessly and without waste.

CLG has continuously been aware, throughout our involvement with the Department, that a fine balance must be struck between numbers of management staff dedicated, or partially dedicated, to monitoring and running their FM Contract(s). If staffing numbers are too low, a kind of management laissez-faire will prevail, and service levels are likely to fall where they might. If staffing levels are too high, accusations of waste are likely to be levelled and will succeed. CLG has used all audit reports on their FM Contracts over the years as a way of seeing their client-side effectiveness (even by exception), and to tweak their involvement accordingly.

The Personal Element

Nuance can be further complicated through longevity, and here simply through long-term relationships with client and contractor. In CLG's case, our firm has known all client managers for years. We know their business well, and we know (roughly) the ongoing stresses and strains they face. We are likely to be continually aware of their overall perceptions of the contract's success itself, and if they do have the time and inclination to dedicate to its improvement/ detailed monitoring.

Similarly, we have known all contractor FM managers from the inception of CLG's outsourced FM arrangements. We will have our own internal views on individual capabilities, of personal traits, and of their management of the contract. We are likely to have met many individuals who have been and gone, and heard formal and informal opinions as to why changes have occurred. We bring to any audit party, huge amounts of non-audit opinions as to how the contract truly **is** being managed and its overall success.

In the context of personal interaction then, having that purely human and personal knowledge and opinions has the potential to further cloud or positively inform opinions made.

In our case, and this would be the same with any professional team who undertake any audit, we have developed the ability to ignore any personal biases. Behind the closed door of any audit situation, we might compare notes on perceptions. Given that the audit itself must be based on verifiable data, and this is the mantra of auditing, personal considerations will always be discounted before drafting occurs, and great pains to prevent that happening is a matter of course.

Discounting any personal opinion, through long-term contact, might mean that the audit report will reflect (to a nuanced degree) other issues known to be occurring simultaneously. If any contract member has been ill for some time (and this has NOT been the case with CLG), for example, we would reflect the natural effect this might have on any lack of progress on a relevant issue. Auditors will never use private information to deliberately hurt, or to allow that information to form an unfair opinion. And this is to say that, personal opinions or information will only be used as a further nuanced knowledge of why some things may have occurred, or not. This knowledge will be a (relatively small) aspect to the large amount of data under consideration.

Summary

CLG's experience of FM auditing over the past 12 years will echo many other Government Departments'. Audits have been used consistently, though not always with a consistent approach. Different managers have specialised in different areas, dependent on their areas of expertise, and on the policies of the day.

The consistency that did exist, however, did and does provide a strong linkage between different contracts and management regimes. CLG probably does prove that, despite the massive amounts of change intrinsic in the public sector estate, having an audit regime in place assists in the running of their estate.

Change in CLG's FM regime was of all kinds – forced, collaborative and by exception. As different FM structures changed, the process of managing a strong FM service did become more streamlined and more able to be focussed on salient points. Given that when CLG started, the Office of Government Commerce was not yet in existence, and framework call-off contracts were largely unknown, CLG consistently used the best of what government policy had to offer, and continued to adapt as changes in best practice and procurement duly arrived.

The use of one firm directly contributed to a sense of continuity in the management regime. However varied the audits were, having one firm who understood the detail of what had transpired over the course of the contract shortened the learning curve for any newly incumbent public sector manager.

As auditor/client relations remained strong, sharing of information remained a strong element of success in the overall trajectory of CLG's FM audit regime. Despite over a decade of consistent auditing, our firm was able to keep its independence, and work in an extremely varied way in answering performance and technical questions asked.

CLG's lessons learned for other government departments would then be:

- a long-term FM audit regime is of value

- audits can be extremely varied without losing the ability to affect change

- a strong auditor/client relationship has tangential benefits for management in terms of contributing to management strength.

Appendix 2:
Basic Audit Models for Individual Service Streams

This Appendix outlines the key audit questions for understanding individual FM service streams performance.

The diagrams that follow are not comprehensive, but provide a good starting point for any individual looking to undertake or commission an audit.

All lessons learned throughout this book can be applied to these basic structures – in terms of subsidiary questions, micro/macro examinations, seeing in the round and so on. Using these diagrams as that starting point, however, will provide a strong basis for any initial understanding of any individual service stream's relative compliance.

Planned Preventative Maintenance

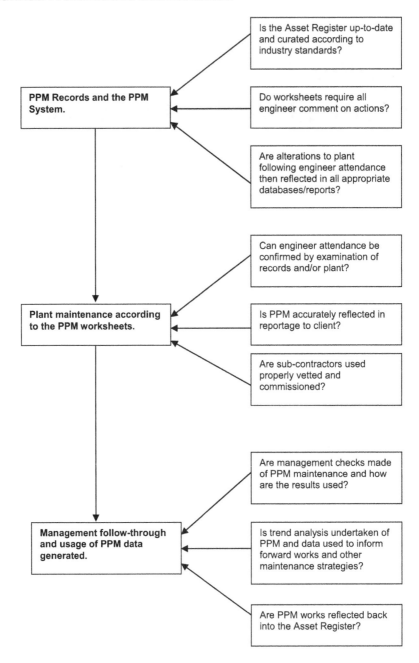

Figure A2.1   Key audit questions – planned preventative maintenance

Reactive Maintenance

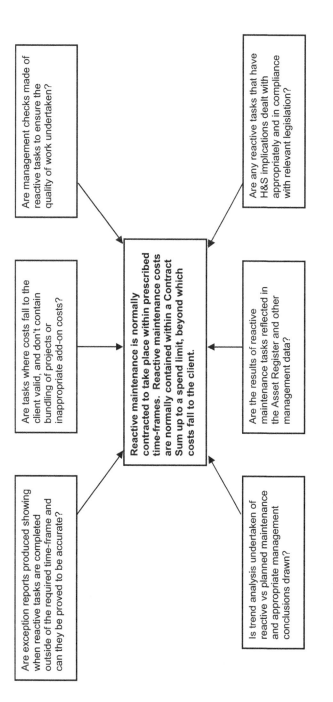

Are exception reports produced showing when reactive tasks are completed outside of the required time-frame and can they be proved to be accurate?

Are tasks where costs fall to the client valid, and don't contain bundling of projects or inappropriate add-on costs?

Are management checks made of reactive tasks to ensure the quality of work undertaken?

Reactive maintenance is normally contracted to take place within prescribed time-frames. Reactive maintenance costs are normally contained within a Contract Sum up to a spend limit, beyond which costs fall to the client.

Is trend analysis undertaken of reactive vs planned maintenance and appropriate management conclusions drawn?

Are the results of reactive maintenance tasks reflected in the Asset Register and other management data?

Are any reactive tasks that have H&S implications dealt with appropriately and in compliance with relevant legislation?

Figure A2.2   Key audit questions – reactive maintenance

Forward Works Planning

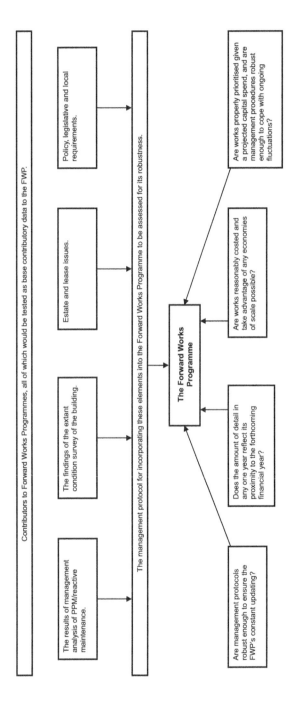

Contributors to Forward Works Programmes, all of which would be tested as base contributory data to the FWP.

The results of management analysis of PPM/reactive maintenance.

The findings of the extant condition survey of the building.

Estate and lease issues.

Policy, legislative and local requirements.

The management protocol for incorporating these elements into the Forward Works Programme to be assessed for its robustness.

The Forward Works Programme

Are management protocols robust enough to ensure the FWP's constant updating?

Does the amount of detail in any one year reflect its proximity to the forthcoming financial year?

Are works reasonably costed and take advantage of any economies of scale possible?

Are works properly prioritised given a projected capital spend, and are management procedures robust enough to cope with ongoing fluctuations?

Figure A2.3   Key audit questions – forward works planning

Health & Safety Compliance

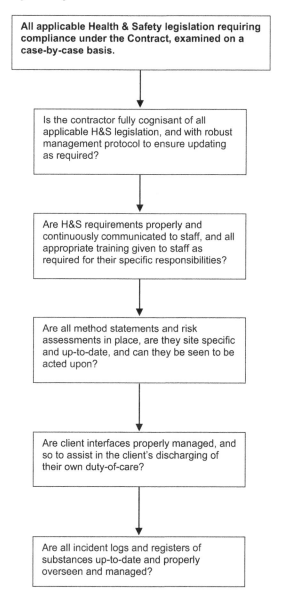

Figure A2.4   Key audit questions – health & safety compliance

Small Works Projects

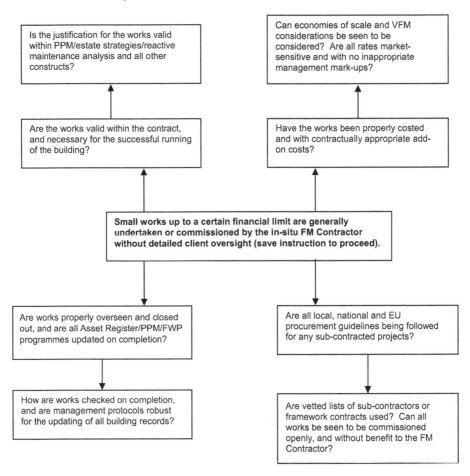

Figure A2.5   Key audit questions – small works projects

Key Performance Indicator Assessment

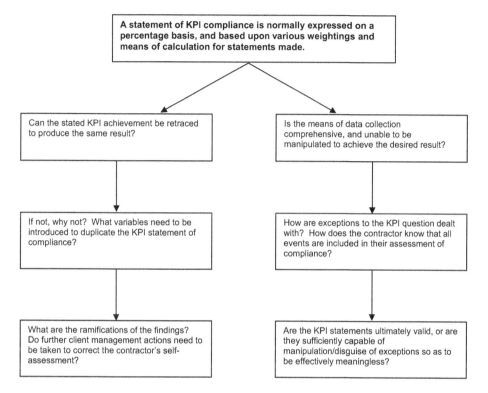

Figure A2.6   Key audit questions – key performance indicator assessment

Cleaning

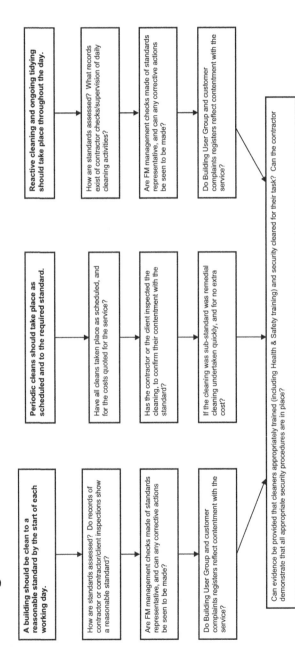

Figure A2.7 Key audit questions – cleaning service

Catering and Hospitality

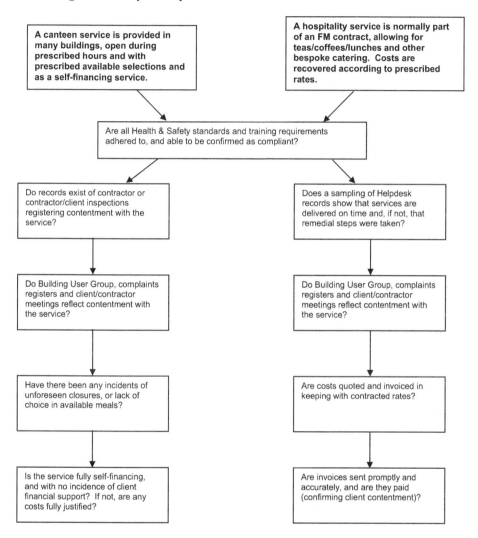

Figure A2.8   Key audit questions – catering and hospitality services

Security

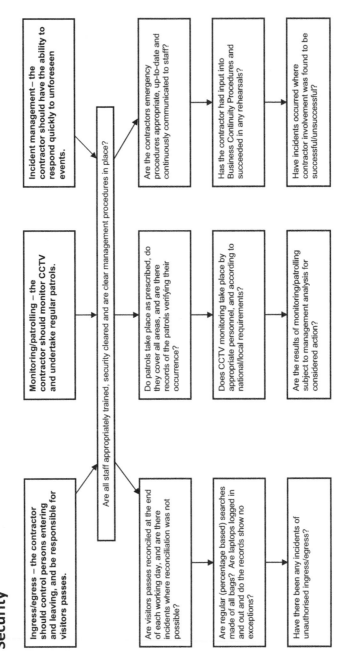

Figure A2.9 Key audit questions – security service

Appendix 3: Sources and Bibliography

HM Treasury Group Departmental Strategic Objectives: 2008–11; published July 2009

HM Treasury Value for money delivery agreement; published July 2009

Operational Efficiency Programme; published April 2009

HM Treasury 2008 Pre-Budget Report

HM Treasury Managing Public Money; published October 2007

HM Treasury Value for Money Assessment Guidance; published November 2006

HM Treasury Good Practice Guidance – Delivering Audit Assignments: A Risk-based Approach; published November 2005

HM Treasury Regularity, Propriety and Value for Money; published November 2004

HM Treasury Infrastructure procurement: delivering long-term value; published March 2008

HM Treasury Taskforce Technical Note No 6 – How to Manage the Delivery of Long Term PFI Contracts

HM Treasury – PFI: strengthening long-term partnerships; published March 2006

HM Treasury – Standardisation of PFI Contracts Version 3; published April 2004

HM Treasury – Standardisation of PFI Contracts Version 4; published March 2007

HM Treasury – Standardisation of PFI Contracts Version 4 – An outline of Principal Changes; published March 2007

HM Treasury – The Orange Book – Management of Risk – Principles and Concepts; published October 2007

HM Treasury – The Green Book – Appraisal and Evaluation in Central Government

HM Treasury – Value for Money Assessment Guidance; published November 2006

HM Treasury – Government Internal Audit Standards – Good Practice Guidance; published April 2009

HM Treasury, Cabinet Office, National Audit Office, Audit Commission, Office for National Statistics – Choosing The Right Fabric: A Framework or Performance Information; published March 2001

Public Audit Forum – What Public Sector Bodies can expect from their Auditors; published March 2000

Fraud Act 2006

National Audit Office – Performance Frameworks and Board Reporting; published July 2009

National Audit Office – Intelligent Monitoring; published June 2009

National Audit Office – Assessment of the Capability Review programme; published February 2009

National Audit Office/HM Treasury – Tackling External Fraud; published 2008

National Audit Office – Good Government; published October 2008

National Audit Office – The use of sanctions and rewards in the public sector; published 2008

National Audit Office – Making Changes in Operational PFI Projects; published 17 January 2008;

National Audit Office – Benchmarking and market testing the ongoing services component of PFI Projects; published 6 June 2007

National Audit Office – A Framework for evaluating the implementation of Private Finance Initiative Projects Volumes 1 and 2; published May 2006

National Audit Office – Measuring the Performance of Government Departments; published March 2001

National Audit Office – Good Practice in Performance Reporting in Executive Agencies and Non-Departmental Public Bodies; published March 2000

House of Commons Public Administration Select Committee – Good Government – Eighth Report of Session 2008–09 Volume II; published 18 June 2009

House of Commons Public Accounts Committee – Central government's management of service contracts – 17th Report of Session 2008–09; published 28 April 2009

House of Commons Public Administration Select Committee – Ethics and Standards: Further Report: Government Response to the Third Report of the Committee; published 20 March 2009

House of Commons Public Accounts Commission – Thirteenth Report; published 11 July 2007

Holding to Account – The Review of Audit and Accountability for Central Government, Report by Lord Sharman of Redlynch; published February 2001

'Audit and Accountability – The Government Response to Lord Sharman's Report "Holding to Account"'

4ps – a guide to contract management for PFI and PPP projects – Published 2007

4ps – PFI/PPP operational project review 2006 – schools sector

Government Resources and Accounts Act 2000 – Chapter 20

Investigating the performance of operational PFI contracts – Partnerships UK

KPMG – Effectiveness of operational contracts in PFI; published 2007

Office of Government Commerce – High Performing Property – Routemap to asset management excellence

Office of Government Commerce/National Audit Office – Good practice contract management framework; December 2008

Audit Commission – National Fraud Initiative 2006/07; published March 2008

Audit Commission – Best value audit and inspection referrals; published May 2006

Audit Commission – Inspection reform: the future of local services inspection; published March 2006

ASOSAI – Fifth ASOSAI Research Project – Performance Auditing Guidelines – October 2000

INTOSAI – Implementation Guidelines for Performance Auditing; published July 2004

European Court of Auditors – Performance Audit Manual

The Chartered Institute of Public Finance and Accountancy – An assessment of the possible application of the public sector audit model to the UK private sector; published September 2002

The European Foundation for Quality Management – The Excellence Model

Index